Caught Up *in the* Counsel *of* God

WARRIOR NOTES PUBLISHING

Caught Up *in the* Counsel *of* God

UNLOCKING THE REALITY
OF PSALM 91 IN YOUR LIFE

Dr. Kevin L. Zadai

Please note that Warrior Notes publishing style capitalizes certain pronouns in Scripture that refer to the Father, Son, and Holy Spirit, which may differ from some publishers' styles. Take note that the name "satan" and related names are not capitalized. We choose not to acknowledge him, even to the point of violating accepted grammatical rules. All emphasis within Scripture quotations is the author's own.

Warrior Notes Publishing
P O Box 1288
Destrehan, LA 70047

Cover design: Virtually Possible Designs

For more information about our school, go to warriornotesschool.com. Reach us on the internet: kevinzadai.com

ISBN 13 TP: 978-1-6631-0209-6

ISBN 13 eBook: 978-1-6631-0210-2

ISBN 13 Audiobook: 978-1-6631-0211-9

Dedication

I DEDICATE this book to the Lord Jesus Christ. When I died during surgery and met with Jesus on the other side, He insisted that I return to life on earth and help people with their destinies. Because of Jesus's love and concern for people, the Lord has actually chosen to send a person back from death to help everyone who will receive that help so that their destiny and purpose are secure in Him.

I want You, Lord, to know that when You come to take me to be with You someday, I sincerely hope that people remember not me but the revelation of Jesus Christ that You have revealed through me. I want others to know that I am merely being obedient to my heavenly calling and mission, which is to reveal Your plan to fulfill the divine destiny for each of God's children.

Acknowledgments

IN addition to sharing my story with everyone through the book *Heavenly Visitation: A Guide to the Supernatural,* God has commissioned me to write over eighty books and study guides. Most recently, the Lord gave me the commission to produce this book, *Caught Up in the Counsel of God.* This title addresses some of the revelations concerning the areas that Jesus revealed to me through the Word of God and by the Spirit of God during several visitations. I want to thank everyone who has encouraged, assisted and prayed for me while writing this work. Special thanks to my wonderful wife, Kathi, for her love and dedication to the Lord and me. Thank you to my excellent staff for the beautiful job editing this book.

Contents

Introduction

WE often think it takes a special people, God's select ones, to receive imparted wisdom and be caught up in the counsel of God. In some instances, this is true, considering what is known of the apostle Paul and others who have reported encountering God's counsel. It's not always a catching-away meeting with Him to receive His understanding; it can be a vision or a snapshot where He reveals His direction that causes a movement, change, or growth. When we make room, position ourselves in righteousness, and allow Him to move, we make ourselves available to receive His instruction. Then, the fruit of our relationship with the Most High God is evident to all, and He is made known through us on the earth.

God bless you,

Dr. Kevin L. Zadai

Chapter 1

Expect *the* Counsel *of* God

I know a man in Christ who fourteen years ago—whether in the body I do not know, or whether out of the body I do not know, God knows—such a one was caught up to the third heaven.

—2 Corinthians 12:2

THE Spirit of God desires to take you higher and impart His revelation. Understanding God's counsel will advance you to the next level. In the Bible, many people encountered the Spirit of God washing over them. He would wrap and take them, and they would get caught up in His glory. They were taken from their ordinary lives, brought into the supernatural realm, and shown what would transform them. They wrote about their experiences, which helps us today. Everyone can encounter the Word of God, so we can all be caught up.

Enoch was caught up because he walked closely with God. By faith, he was taken and did not see death (Genesis 5:24; Hebrews 11:5). The apostle Paul was caught up and wrote most of the New Testament. On the island of

Patmos, John was caught up and saw a vision of the end times. In the fivefold ministry, the apostle, prophet, pastor, teacher, and evangelist should all be caught up in the counsel of God. You should expect God to counsel you as a normal way of life.

At any time, the Spirit of God can breathe on you and you will suddenly receive revelation. It doesn't have to be an open vision or being taken away without a connection to the earthly realm. When the Spirit of God catches me up and gives me counsel, it happens in a flash. I could be speaking at a conference or flying my airplane. I could be walking down the street or picking up the mail. The Lord can give you a mini vision and reveal what He wants to show you. He can speak to you through His still, small voice.

At some point in everyone's life, they go from being called to being chosen. God calls you and explains your assignment; in this phase, you are caught up. Everyone who is called has that moment when God visits them, whether through a prophecy, a word, or visitation.

WAGE THE GOOD WARFARE

> *This charge I commit to you, son Timothy, according to the prophecies previously made concerning you, that by them you may wage the good warfare.*
>
> —1 Timothy 1:18

God wants you to look back as a memorial and reflect on when He visited, revealed, and prophesied your calling. The apostle Paul told Timothy to reflect on all the prophecies given to him and use them as weapons of warfare. In other words, take those words, speak them out, and use them against the enemy who tries to stop you. Everyone is called to a certain role, to work for the kingdom of God.

The chosen part happens when you go through a process of accountability and discipline. At the end of the qualification process, you are chosen. Many people want to be professionals, but because the qualification process is so stringent, few attain it. A soldier is called to be a soldier. Still, those chosen to be in the Special Forces have to meet a significant number of requirements, and many don't make it through that qualification process.

The Lord wants you to be disciplined and accountable. If you are accountable, you will discipline yourself and allow God to teach you through the Holy Spirit and gifted teachers. Through this, you will pass all your tests and become chosen.

RECEIVING GOD'S COUNSEL

I have counsel and sound wisdom; I have insight; I have strength.

—Proverbs 8:14 ESV

There are many types of counsel, such as sitting down with someone and seeking advice or asking for legal counsel. Many levels of counsel are available to help you in these areas.

Noah Webster defines *counsel* in the Webster's Dictionary 1828 as "advice; opinion, or instruction, given upon request or otherwise, for directing the judgment or conduct of another; opinion given upon deliberation or consultation."[1] He refers to counsel as an opinion, which is also considered professional advice. It's an interchange of ideas and an examination of consequences. So you could be counseled and permitted to do certain things, but they have consequences and outcomes. Counsel can have a negative or a positive connotation. The word *counsel* could refer to secrecy or purposes and strategies shared with a few people or one person and considered private. In a spiritual sense, God decrees certain things which are truth and counsel.

> *The Lord warned Israel and Judah through all his prophets and seers: "Turn from your evil ways. Observe my commands and decrees, in accordance with the entire Law that I commanded your ancestors to obey and that I delivered to you through my servants the prophets."*
>
> —2 Kings 17:13 NIV

1. *Websters Dictionary 1828,* "counsel," accessed December 30, 2024, www.webstersdictionary1828.com/Dictionary/counsel.

Jeremiah and Ezekiel warned against those who did not receive the counsel of God and what would happen to them if they didn't listen to Him (Jeremiah 7:20-24; Ezekiel 3:17). In the story of Moses, God told him to tell the people to come to Mount Sinai because God wanted to counsel and visit them. They refused. Because of that, they suffered the consequences. We see what happened to Israel because they did not meet with God. It hurt the Lord (Exodus 19–20; Psalm 81:11-13).

THE TRUTH UNVEILED

In Heaven, absolute truth has been established. Consider God and His truth; He has always existed and is not bound by our laws. He never dealt with time or distance and did not deal with restrictions like travel in a fallen world. It is hard to fathom or understand God from that perspective. God cannot change, and His truth is His personality. It is who He is. When He talks about Himself, truth is being established. That is how God works. When He speaks, He decrees it. Therefore, counsel could be a decree.

When I was in Heaven, God was not open to my suggestions. He told me the way it was and how things operated. I was submissive to the Lord as He presented the Bible, the earth realm, and the spirit realm to me.

We must implement God's purpose, strategies, and plans on earth in the same way His kingdom is established in Heaven. We don't try to redo what God has done or improve it. God is perfect and has established His plans and purposes.

> *To them God willed to make known what are the riches of the glory of this mystery among the Gentiles: which is Christ in you, the hope of glory.*
>
> —Colossians 1:27

God's counsel gives us direction and shows us a preview by pulling back the veil. This unveiling was not invented. Truth is nothing new to God but is new to us and must be revealed.

Paul said, "The mysteries have been hidden until now but have been revealed to the church." That mystery is Christ in us, the hope of all glory, revealed in this day. It preaches to the powers in the heavenly realms. We are preaching to the evil spirits, authorities, and powers, teaching and telling them that this is the plan of God.

Because of that, these powers are revolting and rebelling against God's plan. They are fighting against what God is doing on the earth. But the truth is being unveiled at this time. Therefore, counsel to a Christian should be that God sets you down in a secret place, pulls back the curtains, and discloses secrets. It has always been this way, but we have often been unaware of it. God gives that information and allows us to understand when we ask and seek Him.

> *Ask, and it will be given to you; seek, and you will find; knock, and it will be opened to you. For everyone who asks receives, and he who seeks finds, and to him who knocks it will be opened.*
>
> —Matthew 7:7–8

The Bible establishes God's will, truth, doctrines, plans, and personality. Many people here argue about doctrine and views, but in Heaven, I didn't see any opinions or different interpretations of the Word of God; it was clear and absolute.

It is a waste of time to argue about these matters down here. What matters most is that Jesus Christ said, "I am the way, the truth, and the life. No one comes to the Father except through Me" (John 14:6). It means there is no other way to God the Father except through Jesus Christ. Whether a person, religion, or angel of light says anything different does not add to what has already been spoken and revealed.

The angels, the Holy Spirit, and the Word of God want to counsel you so that you are disciplined, accountable, and walk in the established way. Counsel is ultimately the law, but it is also the way God moves. To know the absolute truth, you must yield to God and not resist Him.

Many people project God and Christianity differently but do not represent Him accurately. At the end of this age, it's not wise to push wrong teachings. We should yield to the Spirit of God, be pliable, and allow the unveiling to happen, which may mean that we have to change because God is not going to change.

ALIGNING WITH THE HOLY SPIRIT

Jesus only pushes Himself to a certain point with people before backing off. He loves everyone and wants them all to go to Heaven. He wants everyone to serve and love Him and the Father. The Spirit will continually minister and strive with people. However, at a certain point, God lets people have their own way.

God has a side to Him where He lets people choose their free will. The angels and the Spirit of God will still be present, however. They will never leave you. They will continue to reach out to you. If you are in rebellion and resistance, God will ultimately allow you to make that decision. It is difficult to watch people reject God, but they can choose free will.

I want to receive counsel from the Lord, and He will deliberately share truth from His heart. That is His personality. He will tell us, "This is what I expect because this is who I am." When we have the Word of God, we're supposed to exhort, warn, admonish, instruct, encourage, and build, but we are not to change the doctrine when it doesn't work or fit into our expectations or will.

> *And, "He is the stone that makes people stumble, the rock that makes them fall." They stumble because they do not obey God's word, and so they meet the fate that was planned for them.*
>
> —1 Peter 2:8 NLT

Christianity is all about truth. If you want the truth, then God will give it to you. The word *counsel* is a legal term, which carries the idea that His truth counsels us. God is perfect, complete, and needs nothing. You are the one who needs Him. You are the one that will change—He won't. You will not manipulate or control Him. He has everything, and you need everything He has.

When His truth counsels you, you submit to it. Do not sit and listen to God's words and get back to Him to decide if you want to follow them. If you are going to sit with God and be counseled by Him, He will tell you the truth. There is no other option. You could reject His counsel, but there are warnings and consequences if you do not listen. That is why the prophets were sent to prophesy to the people of Israel; they were in rebellion and were not listening.

On the isle of Patmos, Jesus told John about the seven churches (Revelation 1–3). Jesus also communicated this message during His three and a half years of ministry. He wanted people to change their thinking and align with God's ways. He did not tell John to compromise and work it out with the seven churches. Instead, Jesus explained to John where each church was in error and gave them instructions to repent, change, and move forward.

THE BENEFITS OF GOD'S COUNSEL

> *But you are not like that, for you are a chosen people. You are royal priests, a holy nation, God's very own possession. As a result, you can show others the goodness of God, for he called you out of the darkness into His wonderful light.*
>
> —1 Peter 2:9 NLT

The first benefit of God's counsel is inheritance. Through the process of counseling, you possess what God has. Jesus died so that we could be heirs of God and coheirs with Him. We inherit everything He has. In John 17, Jesus prayed that we would share the same glory, unity, and love that He and the Father shared and that we would be loved by God, just like God loves Jesus.

He said, "As the Father loved Me, I also have loved you; abide in My love" (John 15:9). You have three intangibles in the Trinity: unity, love, and glory. God has given each of these to us; therefore, through His counsel, we understand what we possess. We benefit in our relationship with Him and from His counsel when we fully accept and yield to it.

> *Abide in me, and I in you. As the branch cannot bear fruit by itself, unless it abides in the vine, neither can you, unless you abide in me.*
>
> —John 15:4 ESV

The second benefit of counseling with the Lord is intimacy. When you sit in the secret place and the Lord shares His heart with you, you can change and be a partaker of all He has for you. This intimate relationship with God is not based on position.

For example, you might have a position at a company and have no relationship with the company or with the owner. In other words, you're just a hireling; you have a job. Intimacy comes when you're included in the inner workings of what is happening. Being a family member is entirely different from being an employee in a family-run business. You have possession, intimacy, and companionship or friendship, all working together.

Some people—Abraham, Moses, David, and Enoch—were called friends of God. They had companionship with God, and He chose to have a deeper relationship with them because He got along with them. If you want to get along with Jesus, let Him have His way and adopt what He thinks and knows. Do not fight the work He is doing in you.

The third benefit of counseling with God is completeness. Since God is complete, He transfers that to you so that you are complete too. You can expect possession, intimacy, companionship, and completeness from counsel with God.

GET AWAY WITH GOD

The environment for counsel is intimate and secluded. Sometimes, the Lord wants to talk to me and asks me to come away with Him. He beckons me to come.

> *He who dwells in the secret place of the Most High Shall abide under the shadow of the Almighty. I will say of the Lord, "He is my refuge and my fortress; My God, in Him I will trust."*
>
> —Psalm 91:1–2

I've had to release myself from whatever I'm doing and get away so God can talk with me. The secret place of the

Most High, found in Psalm 91, is an environment of intimacy and counsel where nothing can come near you and interrupt your time with God.

When God talks to you, He wants you to focus on Him and wants your full attention. During these times, you will often be secluded. The angels set it up and ask you to set apart time to get into the secret place, away from any distractions. Personally, I need to be in a quiet, dark room without any input from this realm. Many people don't understand that. I don't want the windows or drapes open. I don't want anything to do with this realm to affect or sidetrack me. That's why I cannot have any outside distractions when praying, receiving from God, and writing.

Before I minister, I must be completely secluded; I cannot have anyone talk to me or distract me. I do not want an awareness of this realm. You must close yourself off when you get alone with God to receive counsel. If I were to minister to you in a service without separating myself and coming up to a higher place, I would have nothing to offer you because we would be on the same level spiritually. A teacher should be on a higher level to disciple people. That is how the fivefold should operate.

> *And so, brothers, select seven men who are well respected and are full of the Spirit and wisdom. We will give them this responsibility. Then we*

apostles can spend our time in prayer and teaching the word.

—Acts 6:3–4 NLT

The fivefold was supposed to be set apart for the ministry of the Word and prayer. In the book of Acts, the apostles and the fivefold were not supposed to be waiting on tables; they needed to be alone with God. They appointed other people to wait on the tables so the fivefold could seclude themselves and listen to the counsel of the Holy Spirit. The individual has to get away in that place first. I set myself apart and spend a lot of time alone, being quiet. I rarely talk. I don't spend much time with people because I want to stay in the secret place. That way, I can offer something more to the people when I minister.

God wants to reveal secrets to you within a controlled environment. You want to walk with God all the time so that you know how important it is when God says, "It's time to come away with me." He wants you to seclude yourself and create that atmosphere. Sometimes, it's a battle because evil spirits don't want you to withdraw yourself. They want to manipulate you and make you tired. They don't want you to have intimacy with the Lord. They distract you so that you lose your focus. It is going to be a fight.

I decided to do this back in 1986. I remember the exact day and the minister who explained this to me. He was a great man of God and was told to share these secrets with me. Since that time, I have adopted all these truths into my life.

God's counsel flows through intimacy, and after committing to it, it won't matter where you are or what is happening around you; you can stay in that hidden place with God because you are familiar with it in your spirit. You can create that atmosphere without interruption and eliminate the cares of this life so that they don't infiltrate your focus. Some people operate in an environment of drama where they are always troubled. They cause trouble. They cause unrest. You will have to control that and influence the people that could damage your peace and time of counsel. You cannot give them access to you at certain times to preserve your intimacy with God. He will help you in this as you continue to seek Him.

Take time with the Lord to pray and seek intimacy with Him about this chapter. Invite His counsel to minister to you.

Chapter 2

In the Secret Place

Because you have made the Lord, who is my refuge, Even the Most High, your dwelling place, No evil shall befall you, Nor shall any plague come near your dwelling.

—Psalm 91:9–10

EVERY Christian should live and dwell in the secret place described in Psalm 91. The Lord showed me you can frame it, and it will become real to you. No evil will befall those who make the Most High their dwelling place. You must learn to live there, and none of these things will come upon you. You do not just visit Psalm 91 or treat it as a drive-through window. This is an actual habitation where we are supposed to live as believers.

When you abide under the shadow of Shaddai, you are hidden in the strength of God Most High.

—Psalm 91:1 TPT

To understand Psalm 91, you must recognize that in the book of Exodus, Moses, who was the writer of Psalm 91, was put in the cleft of the rock and protected in the rock formation on Mount Sinai. He was told to go in deep there, and the Lord would pass by him in full glory. Moses had to be hidden in the secret place of this rock so that he could stand it. He wasn't allowed to see the face of God.

SEATED IN HEAVEN

> *If then you were raised with Christ, seek those things which are above, where Christ is, sitting at the right hand of God.*
>
> —Colossians 3:1

When I was in Heaven in the throne room, it was so bright, and the glory of the Father was all around. At times, I went to look at His face and Jesus warned me, "You can't look at the face of the Father and live." I could see His form and body, but I could not see His face, just like Moses was unable to look upon God's face (Exodus 33:23). Jesus sat at God's right hand, and I was seated there with Jesus. It wasn't that I was going to die there in Heaven. It was the fact that I could not come back to the earth and go back to my body because our bodies are in a fallen state, and they don't always do what you want them to do.

Your mind, will, and emotions do not do what your heart wants. Two things oppose you in this realm: your body and your soul. Your soul is your mind, will, and emotions, which can work against you, as does your body. However, your spirit is eternal; if you're born again, you have eternal life in Heaven.

When you have been in Heaven and return to your body, your body will act in certain ways, and your mind will think contrary to what you know in your spirit. When you are outside your body and in the spirit, you see and know from a different perspective and are free. Therefore, I had no limits in Heaven. I could operate fully as me. I was fully Kevin, and I was also one with the Father, Jesus, and the Holy Spirit. I was in Heaven but was not allowed to look at the Father's face.

When you are hidden in the cleft of the rock, as Moses was, it is for your protection. Therefore, you abide in the shadow of Shaddai. In Heaven, there are no shadows. It's bright all around because of the glory of the Father, but the light is brighter coming from the Father. The glory coming from God makes it brighter than Heaven itself. God is glowing, and His personality is a cloud around Him.

The cherubim have wings that surround God; if you are in the shadow of His wings, they cover and protect all around you due to His power and glory.

An intensity is coming from the Father's face that is beyond what is in the environment of Heaven. In certain angles in the throne room, those wings will cast a lesser brightness that hits you because of the wings. It's not a shadow. The wings protect you from that intensity. There is protection in Heaven, and Psalm 91:1 refers to this. "You are hidden in the shadow of the Most High." You wouldn't be able to handle the intensity of the strength of God. I don't know how certain beings handle it. For example, the cherubim can handle that intensity, but I don't know how they do it.

I saw many different beings in Heaven that I had never seen before. Some of what I saw was puzzling, and I didn't have any words to describe it. If you are there, the power is so strong, and you are hidden. It is stronger than anything you could imagine.

When you pray, you go into the secret place for counsel, and God is always greater. He is stronger and knows more. The counsel of the secret place is greater than anything you have ever experienced on earth. You will never understand all the counsel that God has. If you encounter Him, you will be in His shadow where the intensity of His glory is lessened, and you will be able to stand it.

HE IS OUR PROTECTOR

He's the hope that holds me and the stronghold to shelter me, the only God for me, and my great confidence.

—Psalm 91:2 TPT

The Lord is a shelter and a stronghold. He is like a fortress. David talks about how we run to Him and we never want to leave because we're safe there (Psalm 18:2). Down here, you're not going to feel safe because you're not from here. Even though you are in this world, you are not of this world (John 15:19).

According to Peter, we are strangers in this world. We are just visiting; our real home is in Heaven (1 Peter 2:11). We are not accepted by the world and do not fit in because we are from another kingdom. Jesus told Pilate that His kingdom was not of this world (John 18:36).

Jesus was a king and had a kingdom, but it was not from this earth. He was sent here. Each of us must begin to think this way and realize that we will receive all kinds of input from God that is much greater than what any one of us could manufacture. You will encounter safety, peace, and counsel like never before. There is no real safe place on this earth because we don't belong here.

Our only safety is in Him. You are protected if He has sent you and you do His will. In the Spirit, this is called the secret place. We are not visiting but live here where we can have great confidence. Moses said, "He is the only God for me. He's my great confidence." In other words, Moses is saying, "I am sure of Him. I am sure of His protection and safety, that He has everything under control concerning me. I am in His heart, and He cares about me." Therefore, we must sit and let Him talk to and counsel us.

> *He will rescue you from every hidden trap of the enemy, and he will protect you from false accusation and any deadly curse.*
>
> —Psalm 91:3 TPT

These traps are hidden, but He will rescue you from every single one. They are not visible, so you must stay close to Him. The only way to escape them and be safe on earth is to stay near Him so He can rescue and counsel you. He will counsel you to tell you where the traps are and what to do with false accusations, keeping you from any deadly curse.

> *His massive arms are wrapped around you, protecting you. You can run under His covering of majesty and hide. His arms of faithfulness are a shield keeping you from harm.*
>
> —Psalm 91:4 TPT

To a lot of people, these are words of comfort; however, this is reality. When you are in the shelter of Shaddai, you will not be exposed because His massive arms are around you, and He will protect you. Your job is to do what this passage says: "Run under the covering of your majesty and hide, and His arms will wrap around you." His arms of faithfulness are going to shield you and keep you from harm. Nothing will touch you, and nobody will come near you because God is there.

God has called you His own, and you've made the Most High your dwelling place, so you are safe. This is the absolute and permanent truth. These are not just nice words to make you feel better. This is supposed to be our story. Many people have compromised because they have not experienced this. They need to enforce this covenant and realize that they are in spiritual warfare.

You are shielded from harm, so do not give ground to the devil. The same counsel Jesus gave to me, He will give to you. People should not have to have a near-death experience or go to Heaven and see Jesus to find out the Bible is true. It should not have to be this way. We should allow the Spirit of God to teach us the Word of God and believe it, but we need His help.

FEAR IS NOT YOUR PORTION

You will never worry about an attack of demonic forces at night nor have to fear a spirit of darkness coming against you.

—Psalm 91:5 TPT

Jesus counsels you so that you are free from walking in fear. Evil spirits are working against you, but you won't have to worry about their attack, and they won't come near you because His arms are wrapped around you. This is God's counsel. We are caught up in the counsel of God through intimacy with Him, which can be interpreted as protection.

Don't fear a thing! Whether by night or by day, demonic danger will not trouble you, nor will the powers of evil be launched against you.

—Psalm 91:6 TPT

Moses reiterates that you have nothing to worry about; demonic danger will not trouble you. Moses saw and experienced all this as God passed by in that secret place, in the cleft of the rock, where God covered Moses with His hand and walked by him. Moses experienced this immediately and had a revelation of God's protection.

Moses took what he experienced and wrote about it for us. This was his experience with God's counsel. God caught him up in the glory for forty days on the mountain. He showed Moses these truths. Then, Moses shared these truths with us. Here is where you must allow the Spirit of God to make God's counsel your reality and your home—your dwelling place.

You must hold on to this revelation, no matter what happens, because it is an impartation. Moses experienced the reality of God. Even though he was disobedient at the end of his life, Moses lived to be 120 years old and hadn't aged nor was he sick. His encounter with God's glory overrode the aging process, and Moses died before the Lord on the mountain in excellent health (Deuteronomy 34:7).

His face glowed so that people wanted him to cover it. His face had transformed into the face of God. Moses didn't even know it, but because he had spent time with the Lord, his face and whole body were transformed. He didn't experience aging like we know it. This is possible for you. This is the old covenant, the Old Testament Bible. Think about what is possible now in this New Testament era.

If we grasp this, no matter what kind of evil is being launched against us, it cannot succeed. It cannot come against you nor can it prosper. Demonic danger will not trouble you. We must understand this truth. Make this your counsel and reality. Sit in the secret place and think about these words.

> *Even in a time of disaster, with thousands and thousands being killed, you will remain unscathed and unharmed.*
>
> —Psalm 91:7 TPT

Even in times of disaster, which we have experienced recently, with diseases, earthquakes, and all the pestilence in the world, this verse says, "Thousands and thousands will be killed, but you will remain unscathed." Moses witnessed this, wrote about it, and imparted it to us. I saw in Heaven that it is up to us how much we experience the Father on earth. We must be perfected in love, allowing Him to do His perfect work. The incorruptible seed of the Word of God must have its way in us. We must accept this responsibility because we are called to make disciples.

First, you must be discipled and then impart what you learn to others who will influence the world. The body of Christ is already influencing the world, but we want to turn it upside down. If twelve disciples could turn it upside down in the time of the New Testament church, what could 250,000 Warrior Notes students do? It begins with making the Most High your dwelling place and framing your world with this truth and counsel. Then, sit with God and let Him help you understand and implement what He is counseling you to do. He says that you will be unscathed and unharmed, even though people are dying around you.

You have made it through some terrible calamities that have come upon the earth. Satan is still stealing, killing, and destroying. Jesus has come to give us life and life more abundantly (John 10:10).

NO EVIL WILL PREVAIL AGAINST US

> *You will be a spectator as the wicked perish in judgment, for they will be paid back for what they have done!*
>
> —Psalm 91:8 TPT

You will be a spectator. In other words, you will sit and watch the wicked perish in judgment. They must pay for what they have done. It is called recompense. This is another side of God. If He says that you are His own and He has enemies, you now have enemies because you are in His family. Your enemies are now His enemies. When people work against you, He will protect you because you are His.

God is saying you will be a spectator to the judgment of the wicked. You will watch it happen, and they will be paid back for their actions. In other words, if people have worked against you, they have worked against God. If they have made mistakes or even sinned and you have suffered for it, God has taken note of that, and they will perish. They will be judged, and there's going to be payback for what they have done.

> *When we live our lives within the shadow of God Most High, our secret hiding place, we will always be shielded from harm. How then could evil prevail against us or disease infect us?*
>
> —Psalm 91:9–10 TPT

Moses is reiterating what He has already discussed. No evil will prevail against us nor will disease infect us. That means we could be immune to these diseases that come upon the earth and seemingly take people out. We are protected, and evil will be stopped! It will not prevail because we live within that shadow, close to the Father, where the cherubim's wings protect us from the Father's face.

How could evil or disease affect us when we are shielded from harm? Moses saw this in the cleft of the rock. Imagine the power of God being so strong that you could barely stand it when God walks by. Moses encountered that and realized no evil could ever come near him. No disease could live in this presence. He experienced this. Moses understood that this was being caught up in the counsel of God. He wrote Psalm 91 to express what happened when God passed by Him. We all need that revelation. The power and intensity of the Father walking by him was imparted to him, and he could voice it.

Revelation came to Moses through intimacy, and it ignited him. He understood that nothing could affect him, not even disease. We aren't exposed to the power of the resurrection in the church. In many churches and Bible studies I was involved with, I hardly encountered the intensity of the resurrection power available to us. People have been robbed, and satan uses these devices and plans so that a corporate setting will lose its intensity.

I have had many visions about the end times where the intensity is happening in church services. It is starting in our services, but the intensity has yet to be turned up as much as it will be. It will begin to happen in greater measure very soon. People will realize what they have been missing and how powerful God is when He moves. Can you imagine having three- or four-hour services where no word is spoken? God shows up and counsels you, your whole life changes, and you have a massive download from Him.

This happened once in Seattle. I stood up to speak and the power of God hit, and people began to fall. I fell as well. It lasted for three hours. You could smell roses in the place. You could hear Jesus. He was walking among the people laid out all over the church. Everybody was on the floor, and people were crying. You could tell that Jesus was visiting them. I think about this intense experience because it was extremely powerful.

When we went to the restaurant afterward, the smell of roses came with us, and even the servers and managers smelled it. When we flew home, it was in our house too. This will begin to happen more and more, but we must allow the Lord's counsel. He wants to counsel you and frame your world according to spiritual reality. In this intensified realm, no disease can touch you.

Take time with the Lord to pray and seek intimacy with Him about this chapter. Invite His counsel to minister to you.

Chapter 3

Protection *in* Times *of* Trouble

We are here for only a moment, visitors and strangers in the land as our ancestors were before us. Our days on earth are like a passing shadow, gone so soon without a trace.

—1 Chronicles 29:15 NLT

THE kingdom of Heaven and the spirit realm of the Father are available through intimacy with God. He desires to counsel with you to give you the full realization of His kingdom. This earth is temporary. You are just visiting. Change is coming, but it has to happen within you first.

The enemy will try to come in and project his terrible plans, but the ones who make the Most High their dwelling place will prevent him. The work of satan's kingdom does not visit God's house, Heaven, or the intense glory of the Father. Therefore, remain in the secret place to escape the enemy's plan.

God sends angels with special orders to protect you wherever you go, defending you from all harm.

—Psalm 91:11 TPT

The counsel given in Psalm 91:11 reveals the ministry of angels on assignment by God sent to you with special orders to protect you and defend you from harm. These angels are assigned to you to help keep you in your way. They are sent because you live your life in the shadow of the Most High.

People ask me, "Why didn't my angel protect me? How can evil spirits come and talk to me and visit me in my dreams?"

We have to live in close proximity to the cherubim, in the shadow of their wings, in the secret hiding place, shielded from all harm. We will always be shielded from harm because we live in the shadow of the Most High. We are to be hidden in the cleft of the rock when God walks by so that we can barely stand it. That is where we need to live. That is our inheritance.

If you are in Heaven and God has a dwelling place and many mansions, you must be able to endure it. I know this because I am already there in my spirit. I was in Heaven and it was my home. I am a visitor down here, but my body and mind can barely handle it because they cannot fully participate in Heaven's realm.

DWELLING WITH THE MOST HIGH

Psalm 91 says that no disease will infect you because you are not of this world. In Heaven, you reside in God's dwelling place. There is no sickness there. That is why Moses would have continued to live if it had not been for God telling him it was time to go. Consequently, God will send His angels. In this step, the angels are sent because you have made the Most High your dwelling place and are not just visiting the secret place. You continually live within that shadow, and the angels are sent to keep you. They are on special assignment because you have dedicated yourself to intimacy with God. This means God is always counseling you, and you are always caught up, so God can talk to you anytime.

Psalm 91 is your reality—even though this seems unbelievable to many people, that doesn't negate its truth. In the age we live in right now, solid biblical doctrine is being forfeited because people don't understand it. It still does not mean that God has changed but that this season is due for a move of God.

God wants to live with us; however, if we don't make a habitation out of our visitation with Him, He must revisit because He wants this generation to excel. If we do not do it the right way on our own, He will ordain a move. God is a living God within us, and we shouldn't need to be revived, but we often do.

If we dwell with God in habitation, would we get sick or have demon spirits attach to us? Would we encounter a curse? The answer is, no, we won't! If God is our home, then nothing else can dwell there. Moses knew this and encountered this truth. But he was disobedient, and because of his sin, he died at 120 years old (Deuteronomy 34:1–7).

God's will was for Moses to take the people into the promised land. God chose him to do that, but he was not allowed to enter because of disobedience. Joshua came and took all the people in. God's best was not done, yet God still had His way. The angels add to this covenant and the experience of God's counsel.

It does not end because you had a visitation or an encounter. Habitation means a permanent place where you dwell daily. The angels will always be with you; they will always have an assignment and a plan, and you will always implement that plan. That is how it should be. Many problems on earth would not happen if people grasped Psalm 91 and lived this way.

The church wouldn't be in its current situation. The gates of hell would not prevail against the church. This is not God's perfect will, but it is happening. We see government restrictions on the church because we, as the church, have allowed these things to happen. If we stood up and were in the secret place of the Most High, then these attacks would not come near us. We permit them when we are supposed to be preventing them. This is our doing, not God's doing. Angels defend us from all harm.

Angels are pushing back and warring all the time. People ask, "Where were my angels?" But it is not God's fault that we didn't fulfill our part. We must constantly be in a place of counsel and habitation. Frame this in your mind, and it will become routine. You must get to a place where God's counsel is your normal, and the angels will be right there implementing His plan. They are with you right now. They need you to continually stay in the dwelling place of the Most High, not go in and out.

POWER OVER ALL THE ENEMY

If you walk into a trap, they'll be there for you and keep you from stumbling.

—Psalm 91:12 TPT

When you are under pressure, inconsistent, or undisciplined, satan can take advantage of you. The angels are there to help you. If you walk into a trap, they'll be there for you and keep you from stumbling. You might still walk into a trap, but even if you do, they will help you through it so you do not stumble.

You'll even walk unharmed among the fiercest powers of darkness, trampling every one of them beneath your feet!

—Psalm 91:13 TPT

Jesus was well-versed in the Old Testament and said, "I give you the authority to trample on serpents and scorpions" (Luke 10:19). He quoted Psalm 91:13. Jesus transferred the revelation from Psalm 91, the secret place, to His disciples, and then to all of us today. It is for all of us now. It is not just for the disciples but for all who believe.

WILLING TO BE WRONG

Every demon and demonic force is beneath your feet—this is God's will for you. If this is not happening, it is not God's fault. We need to be counseled in His perfect will, which means we might be wrong. We have to be willing to be wrong. That's one of the biggest things I have found: God doesn't speak to people because they aren't willing to hear something different from what they already believe. They are already convinced. They have already decided what they will do.

God doesn't waste His time trying to convince people of the truth when they're not open to it. He knows when people become open, and He will let a person go so far; then, at a certain point, they will be humbled and come back and ask for help.

He will say, "Now that I have your attention, this is what I want you to do." He will counsel you. Most people don't get counsel because they have already decided. Some people are not teachable. They are convinced they are right, but they could turn around if they allowed someone to speak the truth to them, received it, and changed their ways.

God will have His way with people if they humble themselves and ask for help. Everyone will need His help eventually, and God knows that. He knows they will come back. At that point, when they're willing to listen, He will tell them and show them His plan and His way.

We must get into a mode where we stand against the fierce powers of darkness, trampling every one of them under our feet. That is the Word of God and what Jesus said. You want to hear the crunching under your feet of the serpents and scorpions. You must realize that these evil powers are powerless against the name and blood of Jesus.

The devils know that this is the truth. They will scream out and tell you. I have heard them scream and cry about the name and blood of Jesus. They know that Jesus is all-powerful, and they know whether or not you are fully convinced. We have Warrior Notes School of Ministry, teachings, conferences, and books to reinforce that environment so we can have the counsel of the Word of God.

DELIGHT IN THE LORD

For here is what the Lord has spoken to me: "Because you loved me, delighted in me, and have been loyal to my name, I will greatly protect you."

—Psalm 91:14 TPT

Moses says that the Lord spoke to and counseled him during this time. The Lord told Moses that because of His love and loyalty toward God, Moses would be protected. You must love God. There is delight and excitement when your whole life is wrapped around Jesus. You want to please Him and hear from Him. You want to encounter Him and get counsel from Him. Loyalty means that if there's a bump in the road or when problems arise, you stay in there with Jesus and the Spirit of God. You don't allow anything to trip you up. You stay loyal to the name of God. The name of the Lord is a refuge. The Lord is a mighty fortress. All who run to Him are safe.

Stay in there with Him and with the name of Jesus. If you speak His name, everything is established and stable. When you mention His blood and His name, demons start to shake, quake, and are paralyzed. They will stop what they are doing and tremble because they know the authority that God has given Jesus. Remember, because you have delighted in the Lord and have been loyal, He will greatly protect you.

> *I will answer your cry for help every time you pray, and you will feel my presence in your time of trouble. I will deliver you and bring you honor.*
>
> —Psalm 91:15 TPT

God essentially told Moses, "Every time you pray, I am going to answer you so that you listen and feel My presence in your time of trouble." Every time you pray and cry out for help, He will answer you. Then, His presence will be so strong that you will feel it in your time of trouble. He says, "I will deliver you and bring you honor." What a great promise you will receive.

No matter the struggle or difficulty you face, it is not permanent. God will deliver you and bring you honor in every situation. You must stay in there, stay loyal, love Him, and delight in Him. He will do all these things for you.

A FULL LIFE

I will satisfy you with a full life and with all that I do for you. For you will enjoy the fullness of my salvation!

—Psalm 91:16 TPT

God limited man to 120 years of life because there was so much evil and interbreeding, and He couldn't strive with man any longer (Genesis 6:3). Moses lived 120 years, which is a full life, according to the stops and limits God placed. That is a promise from God; He will satisfy you with a full life.

You can have a full life and enjoy the fullness of His salvation. The word *salvation* in Hebrew is *Yeshua,* which is the name of Jesus. In Hebrew, *Yeshua* means "salvation" or "deliverance."[2] Moses is saying, "You are going to enjoy the fullness of my Jesus."

It was not just for Moses but for all of us. The best way to receive your foundation for counsel and be caught up is to meditate on Psalm 91. Do it all the time. Daily. Keep it before you and frame your world by it. If you meditate on Psalm 91, it will become your normal, and you will begin to operate in it. Then, when struggles come, you

2. "H3444 - Yəšû'â - Strong's Hebrew Lexicon," Blue Letter Bible, accessed December 12, 2024, www.blueletterbible.org/lexicon/h3444/kjv/wlc/0-1/.

will not be moved because you know you are just visiting this realm and it isn't permanent. The spiritual world and the physical world both operate simultaneously.

Be encouraged and trust that Jesus is your protector and deliverer. He has provided everything you need, and He is the blood covenant. His blood established the new agreement between you and God; the Holy Spirit is the enforcer. He is the *paraklētos* who comes alongside and enforces the new covenant.[3] He is the helper, the advocate, and the standby (John 14:26). He is there to enforce the new covenant with you, even if you don't understand all the terms.

In the secret place, you can understand those terms. God will sit with you because He wants you to be fully convinced of who He is. He will say, "Sit with me. I'm going to talk to you. Concentrate on what I am saying. Don't think about anything else."

After sitting with Him, you will have adopted that mindset from being in the environment of His truth. You will not fight Him on it or give Him your opinion. Be convinced that because He is counseling and giving you the correct perspective, the angels will step in to help you. This is the proper order. Everybody wants an angelic visitation, but do they want to make the Most High their dwelling place?

---

3. "G3875 - Paraklētos - Strong's Greek Lexicon," Blue Letter Bible, accessed December 12, 2024, www.blueletterbible.org/lexicon/g3875/kjv/tr/0-1/.

You can only have an angelic visitation if you make the Most High your dwelling place. The angels have been assigned to you because you are dwelling with the Most High and being counseled. No disease will touch you. You will see destruction around you, but it will not touch you. All these intimate secrets and details of God's will are going to be shown to you, and you will be entrusted with them. Responsibility and accountability come with all this, but it is for a greater purpose.

When I went to Heaven, I saw we were being prepared down here for our next position in eternity. Everything we do now prepares us for the next life, our real life. The real life is inside you and me. I am almost living in the future, qualifying for my next job. I am in training down here, being held accountable and discipled so I can step right into the position ordained for me in eternity. The same is true for you.

Life on earth is short in comparison to eternity. You want to do everything you can while you are here to qualify for the next life. I am not talking about salvation or about getting to Heaven. I am talking about how you have eternal life if you are a Christian and about qualifying and being accountable so that whatever the assignment is with Jesus in His kingdom, you qualify for it. If you are not qualified now, you will have to be trained. That training continues forever.

There is a lot that we do not understand. In Heaven, there is plenty to do and plenty of assignments. Heaven is full of people who want to serve God, and we should have that mindset down here. He wants to share these intimate secrets and details with us. He wants to coach us. He will sit and whisper many secrets to us. He will show us His plans and what is truly going on. He will say, "Okay, if you understand these truths, it will be much easier, but if you do not, it will be harder. Come on in and do it this way." That is the way Jesus is. He understands and knows the Father's heart, and He wants to impart that to you!

PRAYER:

Father, I thank You for imparting the Spirit in this chapter. Thank You Lord, that everyone is established in Your secret place and that You are going to counsel them right now. The Spirit of counsel, wisdom, and the uniting of the Spirit inside them, Lord, will flood their spirits with light right now. Father, all the people are being flooded with light. May they have understanding beyond their years, a supernatural flooding of light from the power of the kingdom of God, in the name of Jesus. Amen.

Take time with the Lord to pray and seek intimacy with Him about this chapter. Invite His counsel to minister to you.

Chapter 4

Increasing *in* Wisdom *and* Revelation

And the people, that is, the men of Israel, encouraged themselves and again formed the battle line at the place where they had put themselves in array on the first day. Then the children of Israel went up and wept before the Lord until evening, and asked counsel of the Lord, saying, "Shall I again draw near for battle against the children of my brother Benjamin?" And the Lord said, "Go up against him."

—Judges 20:22–23

THE people asked for the Lord's counsel correctly and with order, and then the Lord responded, and they prospered. If we are not submissive and do not ask for help, we will not automatically receive God's help. It gives a wrong impression when people teach this.

But without faith it is impossible to [walk with God and] please Him, for whoever comes [near] to God must [necessarily] believe that God exists and that He rewards those who [earnestly and diligently] seek Him.

—Hebrews 11:6 AMP

You cannot please God without faith because you must believe that He exists (which is the foundation of faith) and that He is a rewarder of those who diligently seek Him. If you don't diligently seek Him, there is no reward. Believing in God is commendable, but even the demons believe in God. God promises a reward system for those who diligently seek Him. To believe He is a rewarder is a big step because there is value in that idea.

God can counsel you about your value and the incentives that are available to you. We can find those in the following verse:

Now therefore, if you will indeed obey My voice and keep My covenant, then you shall be a special treasure to Me above all people; for all the earth is Mine.

—Exodus 19:5

With Him are wisdom and strength, He has counsel and understanding.

—Job 12:13

When you sit with God, you will discover He has wisdom, strength, counsel, and understanding. Whenever you think about praying or spending time with the Lord, you must realize that He is the greater one in the partnership and is full of wisdom. He will give you understanding and counsel. He will strengthen you because that is who He is as a person. You can't sit with God and remain the same. He is not the one who needs to change—you are. You are the weaker partner, and you need help. When God sits with you and counsels you, He will give you all you need because of your close relationship with Him. An impartation through intimacy with God comes when you sit with Him.

> *That the God of our Lord Jesus Christ, the Father of glory, may give to you the Spirit of wisdom and revelation in the knowledge of Him, the eyes of your understanding being enlightened; that you may know what is the hope of His calling, what are the riches of the glory of His inheritance in the saints, and what is the exceeding greatness of His power toward us who believe, according to the working of His mighty power which He worked in Christ when He raised Him from the dead and seated Him at His right hand in the heavenly places, far above all principality and power and might and dominion, and every name that is named, not only in this age but also in that which is to come.*

And He put all things under His feet and gave Him to be head over all things to the church, which is His body, the fullness of Him who fills all in all.

—Ephesians 1:17-23

If you want to increase your spiritual effectiveness, counsel, wisdom, and understanding, pray Paul's prayer above. When you read it, you can insert your name where it says *you* or *your* and pray it over yourself. Pray that the Spirit of the Lord would flood you with wisdom and understanding and that a Spirit of revelation would come upon you. That is how I started to receive this counsel.

AN OPEN HEAVEN OVER YOU

Oh, that I were as in months past, As in the days when God watched over me; When His lamp shone upon my head, And when by His light I walked through darkness; Just as I was in the days of my prime, When the friendly counsel of God was over my tent; When the Almighty was yet with me, When my children were around me; When my steps were bathed with cream, And the rock poured out rivers of oil for me!

—Job 29:2–6

Before satan attacked Job, he reflected on the times God's counsel was over his tent. This is where we get our understanding and interpretation of an open Heaven. An open Heaven is over you, your house, and your church because the counsel of God is there. In the Spirit, it is a lot brighter and more powerful than we think; we cannot understand and see what is going on. However, it does not diminish the fact that even though Job was attacked, the Lord was still with him. It was a test.

We saw how satan came in, but more was happening than was on the surface, and it was beyond our understanding. In other words, satan was allowed to test Job. Can you stay in there and be loyal when you are tested?

> *Blessed is the man Who walks not in the counsel of the ungodly, Nor stands in the path of sinners, Nor sits in the seat of the scornful; But his delight is in the law of the Lord, And in His law he meditates day and night. He shall be like a tree Planted by the rivers of water, That brings forth its fruit in its season, Whose leaf also shall not wither; And whatever he does shall prosper.*
>
> —Psalm 1:1–3

Job was connected with this counsel of God. Even though satan attacked Job, Psalm 1 talks about how the man who delights in the counsel of God is a tree planted by the water, and if you are blessed, it's because you are planted, and those roots go down deep. You do not ask for the counsel of the ungodly. You do not even stand in their path or walk with them. You sit with the Lord in the dwelling place of the Most High. You don't sit in the seat of the scornful. Your delight is in the counsel of God, and you meditate on it day and night. That is what we are supposed to be doing. If you do all these things, you will not wither. You will bear your fruit in season, and whatever you do will prosper.

This is the absolute truth. It is the Word of God, so anything else people say is not the truth. Even if you are experiencing something else, this is the truth. Therefore, let's get it right. Let's receive counsel from the Word of God and realize that the river nourishes us as a planted tree, and we have roots that go down deep.

We will always have a supply. An open Heaven will always be over our heads. Understanding and counsel will always be given in the secret place. That place always exists, and you have access to it. Nobody is restricting you from the secret place.

These Scriptures guarantee that you will prosper because you are planted. The counsel plants you by a river so you always bear fruit and have a supply. That is the bottom line. Believe the Lord and give Him access to speak to you. Let Him tell you the truth and counsel you. Do not let lies diminish your dreams and what God has spoken to you. Do not let any lies or circumstances detract from what God says.

> *Lord, you alone are my inheritance, my cup of blessing. You guard all that is mine. The land You have given me is a pleasant land. What a wonderful inheritance! I will bless the Lord who guides me; even at night my heart instructs me. I know the Lord is always with me. I will not be shaken, for He is right beside me.*
>
> —Psalm 16:5–8 NLT

We have a guarantee that God will be with us in the secret place and that He will instruct us because we set Him before us. Psalm 16:8 says, "I have set the Lord always before me; because He is at my right hand, I shall not be shaken" (ESV). We are not moved because He instructs and counsels us at night.

We should concentrate on these Scriptures and let them speak the truth. Jesus knew and utilized Psalm 16. He always set the Lord before Him because the Father was counseling Him. Jesus would not be shaken. He went to the cross and did everything correctly. I was shown this secret, and as a result, I always set the Lord before me. Because He is there at my right hand, I shall not be shaken.

HE GUIDES YOU WITH COUNSEL

Let all the earth fear the Lord; let all the inhabitants of the world stand in awe of Him! For He spoke, and it came to be; He commanded, and it stood firm. The Lord brings the counsel of the nations to nothing; He frustrates the plans of the peoples. The counsel of the Lord stands forever, the plans of His heart to all generations. Blessed is the nation whose God is the Lord, the people whom He has chosen as His heritage! The Lord looks down from Heaven; He sees all the children of man; from where He sits enthroned He looks out on all the inhabitants of the earth, He who fashions the hearts of them all and observes all their deeds. The king is not saved by his great army; a warrior is not delivered by his great strength. The war horse is a false hope for salvation, and by its great might it cannot rescue. Behold, the eye of the Lord is on those who fear Him, on those who hope in His steadfast love, that He may deliver their soul from death, and keep them alive in famine. Our soul waits for the Lord; He is our help and our shield. For our heart is glad in Him, because we trust in His holy name.

—Psalm 33:8–21 ESV

God wants to make His counsel permanent in our lives. He does not want to leave us, ever! He wants us to feel safe, secure, and valued in the secret place. The angels are all around us, but He wants us to receive counsel from Him. He wants to be with us continually.

When we don't trust the Lord, everything we put our energy toward is futile. We must come to Him, and He will counsel us to live in Him. We will not default to our own way. People have gotten into trouble throughout the ages when they do this. In these last days, we should finish our race well even if others do not. We should shine and learn how to operate from history because we have the full counsel of God in the Scriptures.

> *Nevertheless I am continually with You; You hold me by my right hand. You will guide me with Your counsel, And afterward receive me to glory. Whom have I in Heaven but You? And there is none upon earth that I desire besides You. My flesh and my heart fail; But God is the strength of my heart and my portion forever.*
>
> —Psalm 73:23–25

We can establish that God is permanently in our lives. You have to speak the words of this verse and tell yourself that He will hold on to you. He will hold your right hand and walk with you. The psalmist explains that God will guide him with counsel. "You will guide me with Your counsel, and afterward receive me to glory."

That is the summary of all our lives. We will continually have God with us and hold His hand. He will be with us the whole way and guide us into counsel. We can establish this in our lives.

DISCOVERING GOD'S TREASURES

Call to Me, and I will answer you, and show you great and mighty things, which you do not know.

—Jeremiah 33:3

Be encouraged as you sit and wait on the Lord. Allow Him to speak to you, and He will tell you "great and mighty things which you do not know." He will tell you what you could not comprehend before, truth about Himself. Many blessings are coming to you. He will show you His great plans and will help you. There is so much more than what you are encountering.

His kingdom is never ending. He is never limited. He will not slow down. He will be greater and cause you to triumph. He will always be speaking beyond what you have previously heard. It will always be that way. Here on earth, we are on a never-ending journey of discovery with God. Even in Heaven, you will discover new things. It's huge, and so much is going on that you will constantly be in a mode of discovery.

I want God to convey His truth, so I ask, "Lord, help me. Make it clear to me even if I'm hard-headed or don't understand. Please help me. Give me understanding. Teach me and tell me what to do. Show me and help me be willing." I ask and plead with Him to overcome me and wash over me with His goodness so that I can be changed in His presence, established, and a better receiver of that counsel.

STAY HOT, NOT LUKEWARM

Those who sat in darkness and in the shadow of death, Bound in affliction and irons—Because they rebelled against the words of God, And despised the counsel of the Most High.

—Psalm 107:10–11

This is a sad story about why people haven't gone further with God or encountered the prosperity, healing, and all that comes with God being your dwelling place. Remember, Psalm 73 said that the Lord is continually with me, and I will never be left alone. Therefore, God's counsel is with you; you will not resist His words.

The enemy can have a hold on you, but you do not become bound instantly. Bondage has worked its way into your life. When people lose their passion, it is a slow process; it does not happen quickly. The same applies to your temperature; you don't become lukewarm quickly. You cool off gradually.

A battle is happening on earth, and I encourage you to stay hot. Allow the Spirit of God to bring you into His reality. You are valuable, and God wants to use you in this life. Do not back off.

Too often, the Spirit of God makes promises that seem too good to be true. I personally find this a lot. What the Spirit wants to say is too much for me to comprehend. A period of counsel and instruction must come so that you can prepare for God to speak greater things to you. Yet we wonder where the greater works of Jesus are. We have not done these works because we have yet to grasp that the same Spirit that was on Jesus is on us. The same ministry that Jesus did is now on us as the church. The body is supposed to operate in a supernatural mode, but we cannot grasp that because we haven't framed our minds to believe it, or sat and let God counsel us. An understanding comes when God counsels you.

Sometimes, I will sit and let the Holy Spirit talk to me. It is different from what you would think; it's not like I'm doing anything specifically. I have to let my defenses down and let Him talk to me. He will say profound things, and they will nudge me to go further than my mind would expect. He has to frame my mind, and I have to let my limits go.

PRAYER:

Father, in Jesus's name, thank You for the power of the Holy Spirit. Thank You Lord, that You will ignite every person reading this right now. Revive their dreams. I pray, Lord, that You will confirm Your Word with signs and wonders, move in an open Heaven over them, give them insight into the salvation of the Lord, and deliver them.

I thank You for the power of the Holy Spirit. I thank You Lord, for bringing us to a new level of understanding with You. As You sit with and counsel us, You take us into the heavenly places and reveal our main purpose and value. Help us understand Your plans and Your heart for Your people. Show us what You have for us and what You want us to do. Then we can fulfill every desire You have for Your family here on earth.

Lord, let Your perfect will be done. Let Your kingdom come on this earth as it already is in Heaven. May the power of Your love be manifested in this day. May healing come as You stretch forth Your hand and heal the sick. Deliver those oppressed, Lord, and free up the people in debt; give them supernatural finances. Lord, thank You for moving among Your people and manifesting Your love. Thank You for counseling us and allowing us to proceed into the greater things that are ahead for us. In the name of Jesus. Amen.

Take time with the Lord to pray and seek intimacy with Him about this chapter. Invite His counsel to minister to you.

Chapter 5

His Kingdom *Has* No Limits

Jesus said to him, "If you can believe, all things are possible to him who believes."

—Mark 9:23

THE limits are off! However, if you tell yourself, "I cannot do this or that," you will begin to believe it. What is the Spirit of God saying? According to Scripture, the Lord wants us to remove the limits.

Who told you that you were limited? I would investigate because the spiritual atmosphere you are in dictates how far you will go. Often, evil spirits are entrenched in your lineage, and you probably grew up with them. They were transferred to you through your family. These familiar spirits are working behind the scenes, enforcing certain mindsets, and becoming accepted.

This happened to me. I accepted certain lies that were not even true. The Word of God began to counsel me and destroy every false boundary and limit. It was unnerving because I was part of the church and not counseled correctly. Ministers who should know God's truth were not receiving His counsel, so they could not impart the correct counsel to me. As a result, there was an incorrect handoff.

When Moses was on the mountain with God, he received an impartation and revelation. Then, he shared it with the people on God's behalf, but the people didn't receive it. If people didn't receive it, then what about their children? How do you transfer truth when it has yet to be received by the people it was handed to? The children suffer.

Generations suffer because what God has imparted is not being passed on. That is what happened to me. I grew up in a powerless religion. They talked about God and Jesus but described Him as far away and unattainable. Heaven was a distant place. Therefore, they were not sure who got into Heaven and who didn't. It all had to do with behavior instead of salvation through the blood of Jesus.

Being born again was never mentioned, which meant that type of counsel was not presented nor received. Those who were trained in that denomination did not teach this. Even though the ministers went to Bible school or seminary, they were never taught these truths. Therefore, our minister could not impart what He did not learn. He needed counsel and understanding; as a result, I grew up with a small worldview of God, but it was not a biblical one.

My capacity was diminished from the beginning. It started with my parents, who heard incomplete counsel from church leaders. These leaders were part of a movement that had strayed from its original state. We are all responsible for getting into the secret place and receiving counsel, like Moses received on the mountain.

THE DAMASCUS EXPERIENCE

> *Dear brothers and sisters, I want you to understand that the gospel message I preach is not based on mere human reasoning. I received my message from no human source, and no one taught me. Instead, I received it by direct revelation from Jesus Christ. You know what I was like when I followed the Jewish religion—how I violently persecuted God's church. I did my best to destroy it.*
>
> —Galatians 1:11–13 NLT

Paul was not one of the twelve disciples; instead, he was working against Christianity. Paul had an encounter on the road to Damascus, and Jesus arrested him. Later, Paul had several more encounters and was caught up. For a time, Paul disappeared from public view and was taught the gospel message that he preached throughout the New

Testament. This Scripture is saying that Jesus Christ Himself taught Paul.

> *The mystery which has been hidden from ages and from generations, but now has been revealed to His saints. To them God willed to make known what are the riches of the glory of this mystery among the Gentiles: which is Christ in you, the hope of glory.*
>
> —Colossians 1:26–27

Paul was caught up and saw so much. However, he didn't discuss all that he saw. He spoke about doctrine and described the mystery of the ages: Christ in us. He talked about all the "in Him" Scriptures. He said that everything we received in Him was hidden. The four Gospels—Matthew, Mark, Luke, and John—do not share what Paul spoke about, but he went into great detail about it. Paul received his revelation from Jesus, but it differed from the apostles who were with Jesus. They recorded what Jesus said and did—like a journal. Yet Paul talked about all the amazing revelations that he received. What he said and saw when he was caught up in the counsel of God was very encouraging.

We must concentrate on what Paul is saying and understand that it must be fulfilled through the church. It will be fulfilled through the corporate anointing—all of us in unity and maturity, which the fivefold should accomplish.

QUALIFIED AND CHOSEN

And all of this is a gift from God, who brought us back to Himself through Christ. And God has given us this task of reconciling people to Him. For God was in Christ, reconciling the world to Himself, no longer counting people's sins against them. And He gave us this wonderful message of reconciliation. So we are Christ's ambassadors; God is making His appeal through us. We speak for Christ when we plead, "Come back to God!"

—2 Corinthians 5:18–20 NLT

We are supposed to be built up in the maturity and unity of the faith so that the body of Christ can go out and minister. According to Ephesians 4:11–12, this is the job of the fivefold. Paul told the Corinthians that we are all ministers (ambassadors) of the gospel, and we all have a ministry of reconciliation. This means we announce that people's sins have been paid for and that they need to accept Jesus Christ as the Way. Our ministry is bringing people into the kingdom of God. The body of Christ is supposed to be ministers who go into the marketplace and teach the Word of God.

When we come together corporately, it should be the most powerful experience. The focus is not on one person; there is a corporate anointing when we all pray for each other, agree, and fellowship with one another. That corporate anointing causes an open Heaven, and we receive revelation that way. This is what Paul revealed. However, he had to be caught up.

This also happened to John. Many years after Jesus ascended, John was on the isle of Patmos and was caught up. Jesus revealed the condition of the churches and all the end-time events. As a result of John being caught up, we understand and were given revelation. He was shown everything in the book of Revelation, and then he imparted it to us. In whatever way the Lord counsels you, position yourself so He can visit you and have a habitation. Then, He teaches, instructs, and shows you what you are called to do. Each one of us is essential. Every one of us has an assignment.

You are called, but I also want you to be chosen and qualified. You must qualify to be chosen. Jesus said, "Many are called, but few are chosen" (Matthew 22:14). In other words, few qualify. You can change that. You can qualify for your calling. Your ministry is who you are.

Go out into the marketplace and use your talents. Let God instruct you on how to operate in your gifts and creative abilities. Use your creativity to start a business because the body of Christ is supposed to run businesses that meet people's needs. You are supposed to be ministering from your creative side. The world system wants to hire you as a hireling for a set number of hours to complete tasks with the goal of making money, but God works differently.

What if you add value to people, and God uses that to help build up people? If you meet the needs of people and God provides an income for you, that is because you are using your creative ability. It is supposed to be this way. These mysteries have been revealed at this time.

THE HOLY SPIRIT IS OUR COUNSELOR

But the Comforter (Counselor, Helper, Intercessor, Advocate, Strengthener, Standby), the Holy Spirit, Whom the Father will send in My name [in My place, to represent Me and act on My behalf], He will teach you all things. And He will cause you to recall (will remind you of, bring to your remembrance) everything I have told you.

—John 14:26 AMPC

Jesus is at the right hand of the Father, but the Holy Spirit is here on earth and lives within us. He was sent as a Counselor for us, but we are not accessing Him and benefiting from His role as much as we should.

When we are born again, the Holy Spirit wants to take control of our spirit and our tongues when we pray. He wants us to speak the things of God into this realm, speak into our hearts what we have not thought of, and counsel us so we have understanding.

> *Which do you choose? Should I come with a rod to punish you, or should I come with love and a gentle spirit?*
>
> —1 Corinthians 4:21 NLT

In this Scripture, Paul contrasts the two different ways he could approach them and gives them a choice. Jesus's personality is the same; it was established long ago, and He gave you the freedom to accept or reject it. But our desire is for you to accept it. This is the gospel. Jesus went around preaching the good news. When people received it and had faith in Him, they reaped the benefits of that good news: deliverance, healing, and the forgiveness of sins. They received their dead back from the grave.

When Jesus showed up and preached the good news, it was a complete reversal. The Word was confirmed with signs and wonders following (Mark 16:20). Jesus concentrated on the answer and the truth. Jesus said that the Holy Spirit is the Spirit of truth, and He will lead you into all truth (John 16:13).

Now, when a person does not follow the right way and does not adhere to the truth, or when they become evil and are oriented toward evil, they are off track and considered unrighteous and unholy. When the Holy Spirit shows up, if your eyes are open and you are in deception, you must decide: Will you continue this way, or will you change your mind? Repentance is turning back to the right path, changing your mind and direction. It is not one without the other.

> *For the perverse person is an abomination to the Lord, But His secret counsel is with the upright.*
>
> —Proverbs 3:32

The problem we face today is that people are not adhering to the gospel. They have chosen their own way, a crooked and perverse path. These behaviors affect others. The perverse person is an abomination to the Lord, not because the person is evil, unrighteous, or unholy, but because they influence others to do the same.

Suppose people exercise their free will to do evil, and it begins to spread to everyone. As in Genesis, sin originated from disobedience in the garden. Subsequently, Adam and Eve were cast out. Five chapters later, the earth was perverse and evil, and everyone had adopted their own way. Human beings were so evil that only eight people in the world were completely righteous and were pure in their genetics and generation (2 Peter 2:5).

DISCERN YOUR VALUE

So God looked upon the earth, and indeed it was corrupt; for all flesh had corrupted their way on the earth. And God said to Noah, "The end of all flesh has come before Me, for the earth is filled with violence through them; and behold, I will destroy them with the earth."

—Genesis 6:12–13

The bloodlines had been violated; therefore, God had to destroy all flesh, including animals. In the first five chapters of Genesis, most of the people alive chose to live in their own way, and together as a group, they pushed their agenda until it became normal and everyone followed the new norm. We are having the same fight in our nation, and we have seen it play out in others as well.

This has presently reached certain levels in leadership and become a law. Now everyone has to adhere to it; we become slaves to the agendas. That is why God says in Proverbs 3:32, that the perverse person is an abomination to the Lord because they affect everyone else. Now, concerning the counsel of God, the Lord showed me that the people who do not discern their value sell others out.

Judas did not discern his value or the Lord's, and he affected the other eleven disciples, letting down the entire group. He sold them all out when he stole the money out of the bag (John 12:6). The same was true of Eve when she ate the fruit and gave it to her husband. She didn't think that it was affecting others (Genesis 3:6–19). It affected her husband and then the whole human race. Then, we see the entire earth being destroyed a few chapters later because of one act of disobedience (Genesis 6:17).

HEEDING THE DIRECTION OF THE LORD

> *And [in reverent fear and obedience] Enoch walked with God; and he was not [found among men], because God took him [away to be home with Him].*
>
> —Genesis 5:24 AMP

This secret counsel is given to people like Enoch, who walked with and pleased God. The Lord showed me that he was caught up in God's counsel, and that became his environment. He had that secret place where he could meet with the Lord.

Enoch was sixty-five years old when he got on the right track and began to walk with the Lord. He lived another three hundred years while he learned to walk with God in the counsel of the secret place.

God's secret counsel is promised to you; therefore, if you are not crooked but upright and walking on the right path, the Holy Spirit will be your friend. You will find yourself captured and caught up in His secret counsel. But it does not mean that you must have an open vision or disappear for a while and come back or experience these encounters that some people have.

You can walk with God so that you are always caught up in His counsel, so much so that the Holy Spirit can talk to you any moment, and there is no resistance in you for the Lord to speak, even if He asks you to take a sudden right turn when everything seems to be going fine. You do not understand why you must make that turn, but you become accustomed to His voice and counsel and do what He asks.

You choose to be upright and make the right choice in a perverse world. The Lord will help you. Ask Him for help because then you can help others. If you commit your way to the Lord, He will direct your paths. He will lead others because He is leading you. Whatever God does for you will, in turn, help others.

When I was in Heaven, I saw that you can rob others of what is coming to them if you grieve the Holy Spirit. Therefore, never shut down, hinder, or grieve the Holy Spirit in any way. A chain reaction or domino effect can occur if you do. As mentioned before, a perverse person is an abomination, not because they are perverse but because of the impact they have on people.

God had to destroy the earth for the first time by water. The second time, He will destroy the earth by fire. During the second destruction, we will have a new Heaven and a new earth.

I am looking forward to being caught up like Enoch. I encourage you and the body of Christ to walk with God uprightly and get caught up in the counsel of God. We are to please God as Enoch did—a catching away will happen.

LET HIM REFRESH YOU

> *My child, don't lose sight of common sense and discernment. Hang on to them, for they will refresh your soul. They are like jewels on a necklace.*
>
> — Proverbs 3:21–22 NLT

Concentrate and meditate on this verse constantly. See yourself seated with God. Let the Holy Spirit share His counsel with you and show you things to come. He will show you the calendar—the agenda—and reveal what is on the horizon in the kingdom.

He will show you what He is doing. When you stay in the presence of God and His Spirit, you can sidestep and avoid many unnecessary issues. Being caught up in God's counsel is an internal relationship because you have the Holy Spirit inside you.

Jesus was anointed; therefore, the Holy Spirit can come upon you. Then, you can encounter the breath of God on you. Sometimes, the Holy Spirit will nudge and speak to me in my heart. Other times, the Holy Spirit will, for no reason, breathe on me. A wind of revelation blows over me. Suddenly, everything is heightened, and I can hear, see, and sense in the Spirit. It is not a feeling; it is beyond the physical senses as we know them. It is a heightened perception and understanding in the Spirit.

The breath of God has touched me, and it is unexplainable. An anointing comes upon me to minister, which is to teach and prophesy. Then afterward, the anointing wanes and goes away. I always have my relationship with the Lord, along with the inner voice and inner leading of the Holy Spirit. Jesus was anointed by God, and He went around doing good, healing everyone who was oppressed by the devil (Acts 10:38). He had an anointing to break the yoke of bondage on people.

THE SPIRIT WITHIN AND THE SPIRIT UPON

There shall come forth a Rod from the stem of Jesse. And a Branch shall grow out of his roots. The Spirit of the Lord shall rest upon Him, the Spirit of wisdom and understanding, The Spirit of counsel and might, The Spirit of knowledge and of the fear of the Lord.

—Isaiah 11:1–2

The Spirit was in Jesus and also rested upon Him. Isaiah 11:1–2 says that the Spirit will rest upon Jesse's descendants, including David, from whose lineage the Messiah came. The Spirit is the (Holy) Spirit of wisdom and understanding. It was all prophesied, and we know Jesus was the Messiah. He was born of the Virgin Mary through the Holy Spirit. The Holy Spirit was His Father who impregnated Mary. The Spirit outwardly anointed Jesus, and this anointing was upon Him.

Now it happened on a certain day, as He was teaching, that there were Pharisees and teachers of the law sitting by, who had come out of every town of Galilee, Judea, and Jerusalem. And the power of the Lord was present to heal them. Then behold, men brought on a bed a man who was paralyzed, whom they sought to bring in and lay before Him. And when they could not find how they might bring him in, because of the crowd, they went up on the housetop and let him down with his bed through the tiling into the midst before Jesus. When He saw their faith, He said to him, "Man, your sins are forgiven you."

—Luke 5:17–20

The men lowered their friend through the roof into the house so that Jesus could pray for him. The Spirit of counsel can come upon you, not just within you. Verse seventeen says, "And the power of the Lord was present to heal them."

As a boy growing up, the Spirit was upon Jesus; He began to mature and find people to talk to. He spoke to the Pharisees about the law in the temple (Luke 2:46–47). The Spirit of wisdom was upon Him. The Spirit of wisdom and understanding is upon you.

When the Spirit of God is upon you, you have the Spirit of wisdom and understanding, and then you have the Spirit of counsel and might. The Spirit counsels me within, but at times, the Spirit comes upon me, and I know it immediately. I can feel Him come from the outside upon me. He feels like a cloak. This is the Spirit of counsel and of power.

In Luke 5, power was present in the house to heal. The power was the Holy Spirit—He was there to heal the sick. The Spirit of knowledge was upon Him, and the Spirit of the fear of the Lord. We understand this is the Spirit of God, but just as there are the fruit of the Spirit, it is still one Spirit. The Spirit has many gifts, but it is still one Spirit. These facets are beyond the dimensions we encounter here on earth; there is much more to understand. When you sit with God, the Spirit of counsel is within you, but you can also pray for the Spirit of counsel to be upon you.

The fear of the Lord is the beginning of wisdom, so always ask for it. Many people, including Christians, do not pray for the fear of the Lord. I do because this keeps me on track when deception is trying to come in. We see this in the early church with Ananias and Sapphira (Acts 5:1–11). The fear of the Lord was not present, so judgment had to come, and it came instantly. The Scripture says that after Ananias and Sapphira were both dead, the fear of God came upon the church and the city (Acts 5:11).

If the fear of the Lord had been upon all of them, Ananias and Sapphira would not have lied. People would have stayed in line. That is why you must pray from Isaiah 11 for the Spirit to be upon you as it was upon Jesus. If Jesus told us that we would have the same ministry He had and perform even greater exploits, then we had better look at His characteristics and what was upon Him so we can model ourselves after Jesus. That is what we all should be doing.

MODELING YOUR LIFE AFTER JESUS

Therefore become imitators of God [copy Him and follow His example], as well-beloved children [imitate their father].

—Ephesians 5:1 AMP

One of the most profound teachings from when I was with Jesus in the operating room was when He explained the spirit realm to me. He shared about prayer and ministry and went through one subject after another in great detail. I thought, *Why do people want to be like all these other men and women of God throughout the ages, but they don't want to be like Jesus?* People buy books from their favorite preachers and want to model themselves after these leaders, and it is very admirable because you can obtain their anointing. But as I was standing there with Jesus, I thought, *I want His mantle. I want Him to pray for me. I want to be just like Jesus and have a ministry like Jesus's.* It is interesting how we can focus on certain subjects and get off track, but we are not aware of it, so we end up not getting the fullness of what God has for us.

When a person follows God closely and finishes well, that is one thing, but in Moses's case, he did not finish well, even though he started out right. All those years in the desert wore on him, and he could not make proper decisions. He struck the rock instead of speaking to it, as God said, and consequently disobeyed God. It happens in every generation when people begin right but end in the wrong place.

After a while, the warfare wears them out. Be mindful that when I was with Jesus, I saw that everyone should want to be like Him and have His ministry. Yes, there are many giftings, anointings, and mantles, but why would we want an Old Testament mantle when we can have a New Testament impartation from Jesus?

Jesus went into the belly of the earth to take captivity captive, ascended on high, and then distributed gifts to men. I want that New Testament distribution. I want all that this entails. Nobody can truly understand what happened in the depths of the earth because we were not there. All I know is when I was with Jesus, I wanted to model myself after Him. However, we tend to focus on less important things than our needs, and we need Jesus.

The Holy Spirit wants to sit with you and show you what is exceedingly and abundantly above what you can ever ask or think (Ephesians 3:20). He will open your eyes. As your eyes open, you will ask Him questions you wouldn't have thought of before. Give the Lord access to speak to and correct you if He desires. The same Spirit that anointed Jesus is anointing us today. Jesus was risen from the dead, and that same power that rose Him from the dead is in us (Romans 8:11). We have yet to tap into that resurrection power because the evidence of it would quicken your mortal body.

We have the anointing upon us and the Holy Spirit within us, but in the Old Testament, people did not have the Spirit of God inside them. The Spirit of God would come upon and anoint people like Samson, Samuel, and the prophets, to fulfill His purpose. In the New Testament,

God has changed our hearts of stone into a heart of flesh and written His law on our hearts, fulfilling the promise of Ezekiel 36:26–27.

We have the easiest way since the Spirit of God is within us. But the counsel of God can come upon you and be in you. It is like a double portion. Concentrate on it because it will help you excel. The learning process can go much quicker when you tap into the Spirit within *and* the Spirit upon.

PRAYER:

Father, I thank You so much for working in the hearts of Your people. I thank You that we understand we have the Holy Spirit within us, and He is the Spirit of counsel. Yet we also have the Spirit upon us as Jesus did in Isaiah 11. Father, let all the people see that the Spirit is upon and within and that through both of these, we are history makers. I thank You for that impartation right now, Holy Spirit. Open their eyes right now, in the name of Jesus. Amen.

Take time with the Lord to pray and seek intimacy with Him about this chapter. Invite His counsel to minister to you.

Chapter 6

Share *in the* Same Glory

I pray for them. I do not pray for the world but for those whom You have given Me, for they are Yours. And all Mine are Yours, and Yours are Mine, and I am glorified in them. Now I am no longer in the world, but these are in the world, and I come to You. Holy Father, keep through Your name those whom You have given Me, that they may be one as We are. While I was with them in the world, I kept them in Your name. Those whom You gave Me I have kept; and none of them is lost except the son of perdition, that the Scripture might be fulfilled. But now I come to You, and these things I speak in the world, that they may have My joy fulfilled in themselves. I have given them Your word; and the world has hated them because they are not of the world, just as I am not of the world. I do not pray that You should take them out of the world, but that You should keep them from the evil one. They are not of the world, just as I am not of the world. Sanctify them by Your truth. Your word is truth. As You sent Me into the world, I also have sent them into the world. And for their sakes I sanctify Myself, that they also may be sanctified by the truth.

—John 17:9–19

THE Father's plan for the ages is for His family to be restored to Himself. All of us here and those who are in Heaven will be the fulfillment of that plan. On earth, we are supposed to finish the work of those in Heaven who laid the foundation. Everyone in Heaven is waiting for the end of the age when all who live will turn to Jesus Christ. It will be a glorious and wonderful day when we all come together.

In Matthew 17, when Jesus was on the Mount of Transfiguration, He had changed to His preexistent state before time began, and He was God and the Messiah, slain from the foundation of the world. This eternal state was revealed to Peter, James, and John while on the mount. Jesus stood there with Moses as though He were on Mount Sinai, talking to Him. On the Mount was the law, Moses, and the prophet Elijah. Jesus was the fulfillment of the law and the prophets. He talked to Elijah as though He were visiting Elijah in the past. The timeless realm came to that mountain, and Peter, James, and John witnessed it.

Jesus always existed and will always exist. Yet He came as a baby and was born from His mother's womb. Then, He grew up and was crucified. After He ascended on high, He went back to His preexistent state and was seated at the right hand of God in Heaven. He has a human body, but it is glorified. He bought back humanity, but to Him, it was nothing. What He had to do was incredible. The crucifixion was gruesome. Fighting the Pharisees was gruesome. However, it was short in comparison to eternity.

In John 17:5, Jesus prayed to the Father and asked Him to share with us the glory that He and the Father shared before the universes were lit up. God's plan from the ages is that Adam and Eve were never supposed to fall, but He knew they would. Therefore, He provided. Think about this: Father God's love for Jesus is the same love He has for me and you. These three things are revealed in John 17.

That prayer seems futuristic, but it pertains to us now. It is all going to be accomplished. Jesus had not died physically on the cross yet but was already slain from the foundation of the world (Revelation 13:8). To God, it is already done.

The Spirit of counsel involves the Spirit of God being upon you and in you in the timeless realm. In the prior chapter, we discussed that you have His Spirit upon you; that Spirit of counsel, wisdom, understanding, and might in the fear of the Lord. All these things are upon you and working inside you. Jesus prayed that you would share in the same glory, love, and unity as the Trinity.

PARTAKING IN GOD'S DIVINE NATURE

> *As His divine power has given to us all things that pertain to life and godliness, through the knowledge of Him who called us by glory and virtue, by which have been given to us exceedingly great and precious promises, that through these you may be partakers of the divine nature, having escaped the corruption that is in the world through lust.*
>
> —2 Peter 1:3–4

We are partakers of those precious promises and of God's divine nature and we participate in that nature. Peter spoke it and wrote it. When those promises are implemented in our lives, we can be partakers of the divine nature. As a result, we escape the corruption that is in the world through lust. So love, unity, and glory will drive out corruption. We are not part of this world. Therefore, if you are perfected in love, you have allowed God to win you over. The Spirit of counsel does that.

When you are caught up and have given God the ability to talk to you and provide you with input, suddenly, you do not oppose Him anymore. You don't fight—you yield. Everything you need for life and godliness has already been given to you through these promises.

The manifestation of the sons of God will come more quickly in the times we live in because we are being given counsel that accelerates us on a path already paved and proven. It does not have to take as long as you think, but at the end of this age, you will need His knowledge.

We should not need to be revived because we are alive. But when a move of God or revival comes, we do not stay in there, stay hot, or become accurate because of our humanity. We all need help. We are all weak. The Spirit of counsel will show us this and correct us. It would help you to read Ephesians and Colossians and immerse yourself in these books as much as possible.

BLESSED AND CHOSEN

> *Blessed be the God and Father of our Lord Jesus Christ, who has blessed us with every spiritual blessing in the heavenly places in Christ.*
>
> —Ephesians 1:3

In Ephesians 1:3–14, God has given and revealed to us His counsel. The Spirit counsels us to ensure that we know we are blessed. He has already blessed us with every spiritual blessing. How many spiritual blessings have you been blessed with that you do not know about? If it says, "every spiritual blessing," then some are on the list that I probably do not know about. Every spiritual blessing has been given to us because we are seated with Christ in the heavenly places.

Ephesians 2:6 and Colossians 3:1 repeat this: that we are seated with Christ in the heavenly realms. Our focus should be on where we are seated. We have inherited everything that Jesus has inherited, which means we are sitting with Him at the right hand of God.

> *Just as He chose us in Him before the foundation of the world, that we should be holy and without blame before Him in love.*
>
> —Ephesians 1:4

Some people think this verse means that we don't have free will because it sounds like God has already chosen those who will be saved and those who will not. But that is not what this verse is saying. Calvinism interprets and teaches predestination that way. However, we are not discussing that kind of predestination. Here, Paul refers to the fact that God chose all of us in Him before the foundation of the world because we were all fallen and needed a Savior.

This general statement says here that Jesus Christ died for all before the foundation of the world. It is similar to what is written in Revelation, that the Lamb was slain from the foundation of the world (Revelation 13:8).

God always knew that free will would be a liability. Yet He made man in His image and gave them free will. God knew that man would fall, and He provided a way out before He ever chose to create man. The point is that we were chosen in Him because God planned that we would be bought. He already decided to purchase us before we were created and before humans came to earth. God had already ordained Jesus Christ to purchase us. From the foundation of the world, we were chosen to be in Him.

We are one family in Christ, and God's heart bought humans back before Adam and Eve fell and before He made man. You must grasp the preexistent state of Jesus Christ. God's counsel talks about creating man and making them in His image, which means the image was free will. That means God's desire is for them to serve him because they love him, not because they have to. That is why there was a choice in the garden. Free will required that they could choose to refuse.

God wanted them to obey and serve Him because they chose to, not because they had to. He told them not to eat from the tree because they were not God. Only God can know evil and still choose to do good. We are weaker and can be seduced, but God cannot.

He chose us in Him from the foundation of the world because He knew He would have to buy us back. From the foundation of the world, He also decided we would be holy, set apart, and without blame before Him in love. Before the foundation of the world, He preordained us to step into the condition of love. He chose this for us before He ever made us. It is all possible. If everyone begins to receive His counsel and walk in this revelation, how quickly would Jesus come to take His bride?

This concerns the revelation of who we are. When the sons of God know who they are on earth, they will be revealed. All creation is groaning for that day, so we will be caught up when it comes. We will disappear, step over, and be glorified in the twinkling of an eye. That is how it will happen, as it did for Enoch. *Predestined* means that there is a predetermined destination.

Your destiny was predetermined through adoption. Though you were outside the family, He has opened the way for you to be in the family. It means that the destination is available; it was predestined. It has always been available, and we get to choose. He does not take our free will away from us. He gives us a choice. Everything in life has to do with choices.

Your life and situation today are due to the choices you made. If you make wise choices today, it is only a matter of time before you reap the benefits of those wise choices. It takes a while because you are planting the seed of the Word of God. Then, the crop takes time to grow and is revealed. If you don't eat the crop but plant it again, it becomes a whole field. You will receive a huge harvest.

Since we are predestined to adoption, God would adopt us as sons through Jesus Christ. This was a legal transaction: Jesus bought us back, purchased us for Himself, and delivered us to the Father. This is all according to the good pleasure of His will. God's pleasure in His heart is that all this would be accomplished. Jesus is seated now at the right hand of God and is not doing anything else until it is time to get His bride. The Holy Spirit is working right now. We had the Father and the Son, and now we have the Holy Spirit working on earth.

At a specific time, this earth will end, and the next age will arrive. In this current age of the church, the gates of hell will not prevail against us. We will be here on earth, holding back the antichrist from appearing until the church is without spot and wrinkle and functioning in the fivefold ministry, being built up, and ministering to the world in the marketplace. This is all His plan. We are reaching the place where we need to continue and mature. The only way we can do that is to yield to the Spirit of counsel.

To the praise of the glory of His grace, by which He made us accepted in the Beloved.

—Ephesians 1:6

His grace has glory, and through this glorified grace, He made us accepted in the beloved. We are accepted due to the glory around the Father. It emanates from Him so that we are loved and accepted. It has nothing to do with works and everything to do with His unmerited favor, grace, and mercy. It pours out from Him so that we are made perfect and accepted in the Beloved.

In Him we have redemption through His blood, the forgiveness of sins, according to the riches of His grace.

—Ephesians 1:7

We have redemption by the riches of His grace and His glory. Jesus came out of that glory and went back into it. He redeemed us by His blood, and we are forgiven; therefore, we are fully accepted. This is all by His grace.

DISCERNING GOD'S WILL

Which He made to abound toward us in all wisdom and prudence, having made known to us the mystery of His will, according to His good pleasure which He purposed in Himself.

—Ephesians 1:8–9

Paul was caught up in God's counsel and shown the riches of God's glory. It was made to abound toward us—the glory kept building and flowing outwardly from the Father until it hit us. It came through wisdom and prudence; however, it had to be spoken and revealed. The Spirit of God used Paul to unveil it to us. Now we are reading about it. The mystery of His purpose and will has been made known to us.

It was His good pleasure. His purpose was that we would be fully adopted, accepted, and forgiven. He purposed this in Himself. In His heart, He predetermined our destiny. He charted the course for us before we existed. He saw that the glory of His favor and grace emanating from Him would make this path visible. That mystery Paul spoke of is revealed now. It had been hidden in ages past, but now it has been revealed in the Scriptures through His apostles and prophets. Paul is saying no new revelation is coming; only glory comes out from Him when our eyes are open to see it.

Take time with the Lord to pray and seek intimacy with Him about this chapter. Invite His counsel to minister to you.

Chapter 7

Supremacy *of* Christ

That in the dispensation of the fullness of the times He might gather together in one all things in Christ, both which are in Heaven and which are on earth—in Him.

—Ephesians 1:10

THE mystery of God's will has been revealed in this dispensation, yet it was hidden in times past. Because we have not stayed with Paul's revelation, we have aimed too low in our goals and approach to God. We should have built upon what God has done and not backed off. At Warrior Notes, we are not backing off!

The family in Heaven and on earth are tied to each other in Christ and will be brought together in the fullness of time. However, God still wants more people to come to salvation because Jesus suffered and died for everyone. Until the harvest comes in, it will appear as a delay. We need to permit the Spirit to preach the good news so people can harken to it and come in. In these last days, we will yield to the Spirit. The counsel that was upon Paul will be upon us, and we will begin to see the evidence of it.

> *In Him also we have obtained an inheritance, being predestined according to the purpose of Him who works all things according to the counsel of His will.*
>
> —Ephesians 1:11

We all want to know our inheritance in Christ. We know it was predestined, that we would receive it, and it was His purpose. It all went according to the Father's plan, and He worked everything out according to His counsel as He sat and counseled with the Trinity. He may have even involved the elders and angels in this council that made decisions in the eternal realm.

The ones who have been with and seen Jesus and encountered the eternal realm caught a peek at the reality that confirmed Scripture. Then they talk from the standpoint that Paul teaches: the permanent values of eternity, predestination, the plan of God, and allowing people to choose between going to Heaven or hell. However, some false teachers say God predestined for some to go to hell. But God planned that everyone would come to Him. This is the dispensation and the inheritance we live in and has been revealed to us.

Are the messages in your church about your inheritance and partaking of the divine nature? Are they encouraging people into the greater works, or are they speaking about low-level, mundane topics? We have been predestined according to His purpose, and He has worked out everything according to the counsel of His will. His counsel has predetermined everything, and His will was written out. Therefore, we should focus on our inheritance.

TRUSTING THE SON

> *That we who first trusted in Christ should be to the praise of His glory.*
>
> —Ephesians 1:12

There is honor for those who were the first fruits of the early church. All who came to Christ initially trusted in Him; there will be praise in His glory.

> *In Him you also trusted, after you heard the word of truth, the gospel of your salvation; in whom also, having believed, you were sealed with the Holy Spirit of promise.*
>
> —Ephesians 1:13

Not only did those who were of the first fruits trust in Christ, but the Ephesians who heard the word of truth and the gospel were sealed with the Holy Spirit. The gospel was preached to them, the Spirit of counsel counseled them, and because they believed in Jesus Christ, their salvation was sealed with the Holy Spirit of promise. The Holy Spirit seals you because He owns you.

When you place a seal on something, it can mean approval, but it also involves ownership. Consider this: When you become a Christian and believer and are born again by the Holy Spirit, not only is it a seal but a deposit. It is not the full payment. The deposit guarantees the full payment. You are sealed, and that seal is a seal of promise. There is more to come. The Holy Spirit is your certificate of inheritance.

> *Who is the guarantee of our inheritance until the redemption of the purchased possession, to the praise of His glory.*
>
> —Ephesians 1:14

The Holy Spirit provides our inheritance as a promise and seal and guarantees full payment at redemption. When I was on the other side, I saw that I had a purpose and plan that went beyond this life. I had this seal as a promise of what was going to happen. Jesus showed me a glimpse of this full payment. I saw my future and my glorified body. I saw my heavenly job and assignment. When

I left my body on the operating table, I had on a robe of righteousness, but it was just my spirit. Jesus showed me that we will all receive a new glorified body.

My reality was my resurrection body, the uniform I would wear in Heaven, and my position with Jesus Christ in eternity. We are strangers here on earth and just passing through. Earth is not the real thing; it is a temporary test compared to eternity.

Paul tells us in these passages that the counsel he was given showed the Father's plan and the bigger picture from the standpoint of eternity before time began. Paul tells us how this plan was implemented. We do not discern our value because if we did, we would be changed and spend our time differently. When we understand our own value, we would value others differently too. Walking in this will affect others and how we relate to them. As I previously mentioned, Adam and Eve did not discern their value and made decisions that affected us. They didn't know that what they did impacted all humankind.

Judas didn't discern that his actions affected all the disciples and believers. He did not discern his value. Everybody was connected to him. Very few people in the Bible understood their value. They didn't realize that their actions affected future generations.

Elijah went through depression and times when he wanted to die. But if he understood his value, he would have been encouraged not to be discouraged and depressed, knowing that millions would be reading about his decisions or that he would be well-known in Christianity. This applies to others in the Bible as well.

I think about Moses and all that he went through. Had he discerned his value at the time, it would have helped people continue to do what was right in a situation when they were so tempted to give up. I'm saying this to encourage you. When Paul was praying for the Ephesians and telling them this, he wanted to see the Holy Spirit work effectively in their lives so they would realize their value and make quality decisions that would positively affect history.

Whether you know it or not, everything you do affects other people and will affect history. When you do what the Holy Spirit asks you to do for God and are mindful of the Spirit of God expressing Himself through you, you begin to affect people, and they change. Then those people affect other people, and it keeps going. At the end of the age, you can look at the progress through the Holy Spirit on earth and see the result of your obedience. One person's obedience affects a whole generation, but you don't see that because you think about your hard day and how you do not want to go on. You must discern that your destination is predetermined and God planned it for you. Encourage yourself with this revelation, concentrate on these Scriptures, and pray them out. Your predetermined route and predestination will result in the perfect will of God.

For when God made a promise to Abraham, because He could swear by no one greater, He swore by Himself, saying, "Surely blessing I will bless you, and multiplying I will multiply you."

—Hebrews 6:13–14

No one is higher than God, and the strongest covenant is formed with Him; therefore, He affirmed or swore by Himself. He agreed with Himself because He could do this by no one else. The wording here is somewhat obscure. "I am expanding in blessing. Blessing is coming out of me. Surely, as I am expanding with blessing, I will bless you." In other words, "I'm going to associate with you. What is coming out of me as a blessing will overflow to you."

God is expanding and multiplying. Because of that, He will multiply you. The association and proximity with God is counseling you, catching you up, walking with you, and allowing you to multiply to be a blessing. As God is a blessing, He blesses you. Then, you become a blessing to bless others, and then they become a blessing to bless others. It expands outwardly and spirals so that many are blessed. That is how God is. He wants everyone to know and experience Him. You can experience so much that you don't even realize.

And so, after he had patiently endured, he obtained the promise. For men indeed swear by the greater, and an oath for confirmation is for them an end of all dispute. Thus God, determining to show more abundantly to the heirs of promise the immutability of His counsel, confirmed it by an oath, that by two immutable things, in which it is impossible for God to lie, we might have strong consolation, who have fled for refuge to lay hold of the hope set before us.

—Hebrews 6:15–18

God swore by Himself, and His oath ends all disputes. It has been confirmed that we are heirs of the promise. Therefore, God was determined to show the immutability of His counsel more abundantly to the heirs of promise. *Immutability* means "unchanging." His counsel is sure, has already been established, and is confirmed by an oath. He has determined the inheritance and the heirs, which will never change.

Your feelings cannot change this, and your perception will not change this. Wonderful or difficult circumstances cannot change this. It is momentary and ever-changing on earth, but God will not change.

God cannot lie about two immutable things: what He determined through His counsel and His agreement with Himself. It was a legal matter, and all the legalities were done correctly and completely. God will not lie. Therefore, as the Scripture says, "We have strong consolation."

Those who have fled for refuge are encouraged to lay hold of this hope set before us; we have fled the world and never have to go back because we know it is a sure thing. This hope we have is an anchor for our soul.

A NEW CREATION

> *Therefore, if anyone is in Christ, he is a new creation; old things have passed away; behold, all things have become new.*
>
> —2 Corinthians 5:17

Your spirit is born again; this verse does not refer to your soul. Your spirit is permanently born again; the old has passed away, and behold, all things have become new.

There are no Christians in hell. Some people did not repent; many fell away. A person who is born again and a new creation in Christ cannot go to hell because they are people of God. Again, there are no Christians in hell.

The word *soul* is not the word *spirit*. The Greek word for *soul* is the word *psyche*, which is the root of psychology.[4] It refers to the mind, will, and emotions. It is not the word for spirit, our born-again spirit; in Greek, this

4. "G5590 - psychē - Strong's Greek Lexicon," Blue Letter Bible, accessed December 12, 2024, https://www.blueletterbible.org/lexicon/g5590/kjv/tr/0-1/.

is the word *pneuma.*[5] You must be convinced that Paul's message of hope in the book of Hebrews anchors our soul. Your soul will fluctuate, and we will change because of circumstances, but the anchor for your soul stabilizes it. The anchor for your soul is a confirmation that cannot be changed.

> *This hope we have as an anchor of the soul, both sure and steadfast, and which enters the Presence behind the veil, where the forerunner has entered for us, even Jesus, having become High Priest forever according to the order of Melchizedek.*
>
> —Hebrews 6:19–20

We have an inheritance, and it is steadfast, the anchor for our soul. Jesus has gone before us, and then we enter through the veil. According to the counsel of God, Jesus is in the holy of holies behind the veil.

In the new and living way, we can enter behind the veil. This anchor of hope is there to remind us. We are steadfast and stable in our soul: mind, will, and emotions. However, we are divided due to the fall of mankind. Our spirit, soul, and body used to be one, but because of the fall, they are separated. Therefore, you can oppose yourself because your soul could want something you don't want in your

---

5. "G4151 - pneuma - Strong's Greek Lexicon." Blue Letter Bible, accessed December 12, 2024. https://www.blueletterbible.org/lexicon/g4151/kjv/tr/0-1/.

heart. Your body can do something you don't want to do in your heart, or your emotions can even be affected by your body. But Jesus Christ gave us an anchor. He secured us and made us one.

This is unchangeable; this is our inheritance. It has already been provided for us and sealed. It is done. Therefore, we should get caught up in this revelation and remember that God has already sworn by Himself, so He will not change it.

The book of Revelation shows the end result of this. However, you cannot interject yourself into the whole book of Revelation because it only partially applies to you. Some of it applies to people on earth who are not in covenant with God. Some of it has to do with Jewish people.

A culmination of all things is happening. However, prophecy is not for you to determine what part concerns you or where you fit on the timeline. That is not how it works. We might not understand whether it is for this life or for our generation. Some of this is in the eternal realm.

We are still having trouble defining the timeline of what is happening in the throne room in Revelation because it is not based on time. Therefore, avoid being distracted by end-time events or by trying to figure out where we are in prophecy. We are supposed to concentrate on the fact that we are beyond the veil in the holy of holies and our position is secure forever.

THE PRAYER FOR SPIRITUAL WISDOM

I want you to pray out Ephesians 1:17–23, which I pray every day and which you need to do daily for yourself as well. Paul prayed this. Memorize it and be mindful of it because this is your inheritance:

> *That the God of our Lord Jesus Christ, the Father of glory, may give to you the Spirit of wisdom and revelation in the knowledge of Him, the eyes of your understanding being enlightened; that you may know what is the hope of His calling, what are the riches of the glory of His inheritance in the saints, and what is the exceeding greatness of His power toward us who believe, according to the working of His mighty power which He worked in Christ when He raised Him from the dead and seated Him at His right hand in the heavenly places, far above all principality and power and might and dominion, and every name that is named, not only in this age but also in that which is to come. And He put all things under His feet, and gave Him to be head over all things to the church, which is His body, the fullness of Him who fills all in all.*
>
> —Ephesians 1:17–23

Take time with the Lord to pray and seek intimacy with Him about this chapter. Invite His counsel to minister to you.

Chapter 8

Are You Deceived?

And to the angel of the church of the Laodiceans write, "These things says the Amen, the Faithful and True Witness, the Beginning of the creation of God: 'I know your works, that you are neither cold nor hot. I could wish you were cold or hot. So then, because you are lukewarm, and neither cold nor hot, I will vomit you out of My mouth.

Because you say, "I am rich, have become wealthy, and have need of nothing"—and do not know that you are wretched, miserable, poor, blind, and naked—I counsel you to buy from Me gold refined in the fire, that you may be rich; and white garments, that you may be clothed, that the shame of your nakedness may not be revealed; and anoint your eyes with eye salve, that you may see. As many as I love, I rebuke and chasten.

Therefore be zealous and repent. Behold, I stand at the door and knock. If anyone hears My voice and opens the door, I will come in to him and dine with him, and he with Me. To him who overcomes I will grant to sit with Me on My throne, as I also overcame and sat down with My Father on His throne. 'He who has an ear, let him hear what the Spirit says to the churches.'"

—Revelation 3:14–22

YOUR primary focus should be knowing who you are in Christ and having an anchor for your soul.

The book of Revelation shows us how God's counsel speaks to and through prophets and apostles, in this case the apostle John. In Revelation 3, John is quoting a portion of what Jesus gave him. In the first century, he speaks to the seven churches and gives them a warning. Today, none of those churches exist. Nearly two thousand years have passed since then, and most of Revelation has not come to pass; however, this warning did because the churches did not turn and repent.

There is a good reason why everything has yet to be fulfilled. Paul revealed that he wants us to have God's counsel to understand. As he told the Thessalonians, "There is one holding back the antichrist from coming into full power" (2 Thessalonians 2:7, my paraphrase). The word *one* here refers to the church because we still remain here on earth.

We are in the church age where the Holy Spirit is within us. Until the church is removed, we won't go into the next phase. Once we are gone, lawlessness will reign, and suddenly, what was spoken of in Revelation will happen because there is no one to keep it back.

Of course, the Holy Spirit will still be on earth, but He won't be within anyone. We will be in this church age until the catching away when the body of Christ walks into glory.

The same warning Jesus spoke to the seven churches is for us. Therefore, we should concentrate on our spiritual temperature rather than where we fit into prophecy and everything mentioned in Revelation, Daniel, and Ezekiel. We are still to focus on the words of Jesus to the churches because of the condition of the church. All that is supposed to happen with the antichrist is still pending, up to chapters 3 and 4 of Revelation when we transition out of the church age.

JUDGE YOURSELVES AND STAY EFFECTIVE

The mystery which has been hidden from ages and from generations, but now has been revealed to His saints. To them God willed to make known what are the riches of the glory of this mystery among the Gentiles: which is Christ in you, the hope of glory.

—Colossians 1:26–27

To be caught up in God's counsel is to discern where we are and are not effective. Paul told the Thessalonians that if you don't work, you don't eat (2 Thessalonians 3:10). They thought Jesus was coming and had become ineffective. Paul was essentially saying, "He's not coming until certain events happen." They haven't happened yet. They will not occur while we are here on earth (2 Thessalonians 2:3–4).

In 2 Thessalonians 2:6 NIV, referring to the antichrist, Paul says, "And now you know what is holding him back, so that he may be revealed at the proper time." He assumed they knew it was them. This is still how it is today, two thousand years later. We are still in Revelation 3, and we must read it and ask ourselves, "Am I lukewarm?"

Jesus wants to spew the lukewarm out of His mouth (Revelation 3:16). This is how we should judge ourselves lest we be judged (1 Corinthians 11:31). Obviously, the seven churches did not judge themselves because they are no longer here. These exact words are being spoken to us.

At Warrior Notes, we will move on, grow, and mature. We will not be stagnant but realize that the world cannot go into the bowls of wrath and seals yet, Meanwhile, we must watch our temperature and be mindful that we are the body of Christ on earth. We are the ministry of Jesus Christ. We are His voice and must represent Him and get people saved. We are supposed to preach the gospel so that people receive deliverance, are healed, and are raised from the dead. We must announce that their sins are forgiven.

In Revelation, through John, Jesus told us that deception is operating. The Lord wants to counsel us because we do not always discern where we are, and at certain times, we get off track. At times, people need to be told what's happening, and God needs to intervene.

We are ripe for another move of God because the Spirit of God is now moving in revelation, but He's showing the church that we are here, we are lukewarm, and we must change. The only way change will come is if people receive the revelation of their condition. Jesus had to tell John to tell the Laodiceans; "You say you're rich, but you are really poor. You say you're well clothed, but you're really naked." That's a wake-up call. He was quoting what they were saying. He told them, "You say you can see, but you're blind." That's another wake-up call. Jesus Christ was telling them that they were blind when they thought they could see. He said, "He who has ears to hear, let him hear what the Spirit is saying." He is still saying that today.

BE THE SOLUTION

You might be deceived and need God to tell you that you're deceived. Jesus had to ask John to tell this church about their actual condition: that they were deceived. That's quite a wake-up call. But that's what is happening right now. A wake-up call is coming, and you must ask the right question: Am I deceived?

Should you know something that you do not know? Do you think you know something, but you really don't? Are you believing the wrong things? Are you looking for the wrong things, yet you think they are right? You think you desire something, and it might be off. What should you be looking for and desiring? The only way you can do this appropriately is to have counsel from God about the future, which God must show you. He must show you the plan and how you fit into it from the beginning. You will see that you must be part of the solution, not the problem.

If you focus on and sensationalize the book of Revelation, which many ministers do, you rob people of their deliverance and healing. You are robbing God of the progress of the maturation of the church. If you concentrate on end-time and current events, you are not feeding the people and building them up for maturity; you're just informing them about the news. That will get you into a negative loop, where you are waiting for the next bad thing to happen. Every generation has done that, but it slows down the progress of the body of Christ.

We should already be in glory. The gospel should have been preached, and people should have already come in. The harvest should have come, but it delays because we are waiting for something to happen that has already happened. We're waiting for all the prophecies in Revelation and the Bible to be fulfilled.

Paul says the mystery has been revealed and that Christ in you is the hope of glory (Colossians 1:27). He didn't speak about end-time events or focus on end-time prophecy. He told Timothy what people would be like before the end came. Paul didn't talk about Ezekiel or Daniel. What was important to him was Jesus Christ and Him crucified. At the end of his career, he was in essence telling us, "This is the only thing I know that matters."

This was not the study of end-time events. Paul was sold on the fact that everything had already happened in the Spirit and that we need to rise up in this revelation. The counsel of God will bring you into revelation. I believe this is happening to you; you're beginning to realize in your spirit that the Lord could show you blind spots as you are being counseled. I expect this to happen every day.

CHANGE IS NECESSARY FOR GROWTH

If God has to rebuke or chasten us, He will do it because He loves us. He will show us if we are deceived. You must be willing to hear that. Many people don't want to know. Honestly, who do you know who wants to be told they are wrong?

We have a defense mechanism that resists correction. Because of that, we don't discern our value and don't want to improve or change because it is uncomfortable. If someone gives their input and we have to change, it is very uncomfortable because our goal is to be stable and feel comfortable.

We are constantly working to feel balanced as though everything is going smoothly in life; then, an outside situation arises that upsets us and puts us in a bad situation so that we lose our equilibrium. I would rather know by the Lord Jesus Christ if I were lukewarm; I want Him to tell me what steps to take to get spiritually hot. When I seek His counsel, He tells me what I need to know to get there. When we are lukewarm, we face repercussions in the spirit. The Lord has told me, "You've decided this."

In 2022, I had a visitation with Jesus. He sat with me face to face and told me we were going to the next phase and that everything would change. "Ministry as you know it will change." He told me things that were hard for me to believe would happen. They have all happened in the last two years. It seemed impossible, but I have seen what He told me about every day since then. He said there would be a separation. That has already happened.

He told me some things that made me uncomfortable. I realized I have been alone, yet I have been with many people, and I have learned to live in both situations. Either way, I've learned to find comfort. However, at times, Jesus will require you to get hot, and some people won't be able to come along on the journey. Warrior Notes and Warrior Notes School of Ministry were formed out of this.

I am creating an atmosphere where the temperature is hot, making it easy for people to enter. Then, you must maintain your own temperature by studying and completing your lessons, teaching yourself, and helping others.

Your friends will respond differently; therefore, some of them cannot go further with you. Suddenly, you might feel like you don't fit in anymore with certain churches or ministry associations. The temperature has been turned up in your life. People won't automatically go with you on that journey. If they do not operate in that Spirit of counsel, they will not experience what you are experiencing.

Over the years, throughout my education and in all my graduating classes, I have seen many people called and trained for the ministry. However, I can only name three to five people that I was in school with who are still in the ministry. Thousands of people I know of are no longer in public ministry. I've searched for my friends and cannot find them anywhere. There is no sign of fruit in their lives, but they were the most wonderful friends and people.

The Lord called me alone in college; He wanted me to fast and pray. During this time of fasting, He instructed me to tell people I could no longer hang out with them and that I had other responsibilities. The amount of resistance I received from some of them was amazing. They were responding from their souls because they could not understand the Lord was drawing me away.

In my second year of college, I wondered, *What if I hadn't done it?* An angel appeared to me and explained what my friends would do for me and what the Lord would do for me. I made that choice to pull away.

I don't have relationships with those people anymore because I can't find them. Only a few are doing the work of the ministry and doing great things for the Lord, but those people went on in their calling and were set apart. When you talk to them, they are doing what the Holy Spirit is telling them.

Warrior Notes students will go on to fulfill the calling of the Lord in their lives and stay in ministry. At the time of the writing of this book, we have over 40,000 students. I believe that I won't lose any of you, that all of you will go forth and not have to go through the sifting that my friends in ministry school went through. They were unsure of some things you should be sure of.

I created an environment where I could hear from the Lord by fasting, praying, and pulling myself away. This kept me strong in times of being alone. The Lord told me the truth about myself. He put me through so many different situations. Then He put me in a job for thirty years that showed me that without Him, I am nothing.

He showed me my weaknesses, then came in with His strength and counseled me. I constantly asked Him to show me and not let me be deceived. For forty-three years, my prayer has been, "Show me, Lord. Help me in my weakness. Show me exactly what I need to know, and counsel me on this. I want to know the truth."

GO FORTH AND APPLY HIS COUNSEL

The Spirit of God wants to tell you the truth so that you do not perish early, become lukewarm, and leave the ministry. God needs voices on earth. He needs prophets and prophetesses to prophesy. He needs apostles to go and establish the works as Jesus did. He needs teachers to teach, pastors to pastor, and evangelists to do miracles, signs, and wonders and proclaim the gospel.

He also needs the body of Christ to be built up and go into the marketplace, own everything, and preach the good news. This is not the time for darkness to win. In that second year of college when the Lord told me to set myself apart, I got caught up in the counsel of God. It was amazing. During that time, the Lord showed me truth. I was a brand-new Christian. Now, I am seeing the fruit of that pulling away. I had an angelic visitation that year, and the angel told me that I had done the right thing and would make it because I obeyed the Lord.

I think about the thousands of people I cannot find anymore. I expected them to be doing mighty works for

God, yet I could only find three or four people doing the work of the Lord. Out of the thousands that were in other countries doing mighty works, most of them have disappeared off the map. It is not God's will, but that will not happen to you.

Take time with the Lord to pray and seek intimacy with Him about this chapter. Invite His counsel to minister to you.

Chapter 9

The Surrendered Heart

The sacrifices of God are a broken spirit, A broken and a contrite heart—These, O God, You will not despise.

—Psalm 51:17

MY one decision to be counseled by God produced all of the fruit of Warrior Notes Ministries. I want to encourage you to stay with God, allow Him to counsel you, and reap the benefits of that decision.

If we decide we will not be deceived and will instead ask God for help, God will counsel us, and there will be no delay. James talks about how if we ask for wisdom, we will receive it from on high (James 1:5). He says that God is counseling us from the eternal realm and that He is the Father of lights (James 1:17).

When I was in Heaven, there were no shadows. Wisdom is the light that comes and dispels darkness. That is why James said wisdom comes down from the Father of lights. Wisdom is dispelling darkness. Down here, we have a wrong perspective, focus on what is wrong, and end up lukewarm because our understanding of God is wrong.

God is light. When He shows up, there is no shadow or darkness, so there is no misunderstanding. When the angels have shown up and God has taken me and shown me truth, I don't have any questions. Every time that I encounter Jesus, I can't think of anything to ask.

At times, He has allowed me to ask questions, and I was given access. However, I don't have any questions when I am in Heaven because there is no darkness or doubt. God says that if you ask for wisdom, you will be counseled. James guarantees that. You will need qualifications for this, but I have found that the most profound things that have ever happened to me have not been when I was strong or when life was going well. Everything that has ever happened to me was a memorial where God visited me. During these tough times, I had to count the cost and obey God. Then, He came in and accommodated me in that decision. Until then, I didn't have the counsel that I needed. I was broken. I was in need. Unfortunately, this is what we experience in this fallen world.

We think we can do it on our own. We ask God to help us with whatever is pending at the time, but we don't let Him into our finances, and then, when our finances get messed up, suddenly, we want to turn them over to Him and ask Him to fix them. We should have let Him into our finances to begin with. It is the same way with our health; we should always let Him into our health, not only when we are sick. We should always give Him access.

> *"I have seen what they do, but I will heal them anyway! I will lead them. I will comfort those who mourn, bringing words of praise to their lips. May they have abundant peace, both near and far," says the Lord, who heals them.*
>
> —Isaiah 57:18–19 NLT

These verses in Isaiah reveal the qualifications for encountering God. I know you qualify! It is not done in your strength. If you are waiting to get into the right position with God to have an encounter with Him or an answered prayer, that is not how it works. It works when you're broken and have no way out except for Him to help you. That's the good news.

HE RESTORES AND REVIVES

> *The high and lofty one who lives in eternity, the Holy One, says this: "I live in the high and holy place with those whose spirits are contrite and humble. I restore the crushed spirit of the humble*

and revive the courage of those with repentant hearts.

—Isaiah 57:15 NLT

According to this verse, God dwells in two different places. He is the Most High, the high and lofty one, who lives in eternity. However, He dwells in another place: with those whose spirits are contrite and humble. It is the opposite of how the world trains you to be successful. The contrite and humble ones get trampled on in the eyes of the world, but God dwells with them.

If you need help or ask for help and are contrite, then you aren't prideful. You don't think of yourself as being all that. You are humble. Both now and in eternity, God will come to dwell with you in the same manner as He dwells as the high and lofty One in Heaven.

God's light dispels darkness, and you want Him to come to live with you. This is how you will gain wisdom and not be deceived. You must have God come in and dispel the darkness because the darkness will be there unless God shows up.

He says, "I'm going to restore the crushed spirit of the humble." So if you've been humbled and you are broken, God will come to dwell with you, but He will also restore your crushed spirit and revive your courage. If you are contrite, shaking, and need help, God will come to dwell with you. Then, He will turn that contriteness into courage.

He will do that for those with repentant hearts. Very few encounter this counsel and revival. When God moved throughout history, He did not move with everyone.

Once, a revival at a certain church lasted for several years. They were part of a huge worldwide denomination—it was intense. The fruit of it was powerful repentance. Many souls were saved. I was a part of the denomination at one point, but they did not participate in that movement, and it did not spread throughout that denomination.

If you look at all the people called revivalists, they came out of an established religion, but they were rejected. Then, the movement that came after they left that establishment resulted in the formation of another establishment. Now, they are all dead and not participating in what the originator began.

All this is key to being caught up in the counsel of God because the light of God comes in to dispel darkness. He not only wants to come and live with you but to restore you; the broken condition that brought God there will be fixed. If you are battered, crushed, discouraged, depressed, and don't know what to do, God will come and dwell with you. That is why the verse in Isaiah says He will "revive the courage of those with repentant hearts."

CHANGE PRODUCES GROWTH

For I will not fight against you forever; I will not always be angry. If I were, all people would pass away—all the souls I have made. I was angry, so I punished these greedy people. I withdrew from them, but they kept going on their own stubborn way.

—Isaiah 57:16–17 NLT

God is telling us, "I'm not going to remain this way because people won't be able to live past a certain point if I'm always angry." He comes to restore you through Jesus Christ.

Jesus purchased us, and God is not angry with people and their sins. Jesus Christ took that upon Himself. That's done, and we're in the age of the church and proclamation of the good news. That will continue until the harvest comes in, and then, at a certain point, it will end.

After chapter 4 of Revelation, you will see everything quickly come to pass. The saints will walk over and get caught up. Until then, the antichrist is forbidden to manifest in his person and is being held back. The Holy Spirit is in us, and we have His counsel within, which is why we are here. If you stay stubborn, you will resist the Holy Spirit, but if you yield and say, "Lord, in my weakness, you make me strong. Come in and lift me up," then you will experience change. This is because His counsel came in, and God revealed the truth. The Spirit of truth wants to show and lead you into all truth. Once you see the truth, it might mean that you have to change.

This becomes very uncomfortable. You will have to make this decision either way: now or at the end of your life. God will require that you give an account of what you did in the flesh.

THE DAMASCUS EXPERIENCE

Paul the apostle was killing Christians, and God had to stop him on the road to Damascus. If you recall, Paul was working against God in what he was doing, but Paul thought he was doing the right thing, the work of God. He thought these Christians were working against the system that God set up through Moses. When Jesus came, the Pharisees feared Him because He had a lot of influence, the people loved Him, and He spoke the truth from God. He became a threat, so they killed Him. Paul was killing Christians and having them killed for the very same reason. However, they were all resisting God, but they thought they were doing God's will. Jesus said to the disciples, "The hour is coming when whoever kills you will think he is offering service to God" (John 16:2 ESV).

On the road to Damascus, Paul was caught up in God's counsel and given a way out of his wrong direction. It was a gift. Most of us would end up in hell for what he did. He was given the road to Damascus experience, and it saved him. Otherwise, he would have gone to hell.

God chose us and brought us to that knowledge as though we experienced what Paul did before ever going to hell. He saved us, and now we get to create an atmosphere to witness. We get to compel people to come to know the Lord by telling them the truth so that they see it. It can be difficult for people who want to feel comfortable and maintain their lives. They don't want to make waves; they want to survive. The problem is, if they don't make this decision now, then by default, they will go to hell. But it is not God's will for anyone to go to hell.

PRAYER FRUIT

> *If you abide in Me, and My words abide in you, you will ask what you desire, and it shall be done for you. By this My Father is glorified, that you bear much fruit; so you will be My disciples.*
>
> —John 15:7–8

Once the encounter of God comes and dwells with you, you will have a process of maintaining it. God dwells with you because you are repentant, contrite, and humble in spirit. He dwells with and restores you; then you will maintain it to remain in it. People always ask, "How can I continue to walk in this?" When they experience the power of God, they are often left to themselves and don't seem to do well. They might not have churches where they can be discipled or where the power of God is present. It is not always easy, but you must be able to walk in it yourself by engaging with the Lord and focusing on Him. With the counsel of God, you will walk with Him by meditating on the fact that you are connected through the vine.

You are the branch that receives the constant life flow. His words flow into you from the vine into the branches. When that word flows through you, you manifest and produce fruit. John 15 is about bearing fruit through prayer. You are going to produce fruit and have answered prayers. "If you abide in Me, and My words abide in you, you will ask what you desire, and it shall be done for you" (John 15:7). It is prayer: whatever you ask in prayer, it shall be done for you (Mark 11:24). "Whatever you ask" is the prayer, and "it shall be done" is the answered prayer.

When you ask, you receive. Why? Because you are connected to the vine, and His words abide in you. As His words abide in you, that storehouse of words comes out of your mouth. It goes from the spiritual into the physical realm because when you speak, it is audible. Once you release it, you receive it because the word produces fruit. Then you have the physical manifestation of answered prayer.

What happens to you in this realm is made manifest, and people see it. This is the definition of *ministry*. When people see it, you are testifying. You are a witness. You don't go out and witness. You are a witness because people see it. When you testify, it's a testimony.

It will happen "so that the Father can be glorified and that you bear much fruit so that you will be my disciples." The disciples knew they were His disciples because they bore fruit. The fruit is part of the testimony, answered prayer.

When I worked at Southwest, I saw the evidence of the fruit of my prayers all the time. My coworkers asked me about God and various aspects of my experiences. I would say, "I am believing that this will happen, and I'm praying right now about it."

Then, they witnessed my prayers being answered. They saw God's favor and said, "How did that happen?" They (these unsaved people) attributed it to God's blessing on my life. They said, "God likes you." Their interpretation of God's answer to my prayer is seen in John 15:8 ESV. "By this My Father is glorified, that you bear much fruit and so prove to be My disciples." That fruit, as I said, is prayer fruit—answered prayer.

We all want answered prayers. But it is more than getting what you have asked for. It is about your Father being glorified. This is the counsel of God. When you are caught up in this, you walk in it, and you will see these manifestations. That's how you get to the next step. It is not just about sitting in the secret place and God telling you and showing you everything—the implementation is revealed in this verse. It is the most important part of being caught up in the counsel of God. It's receiving the counsel and the manifestation of answered prayers.

> *These things I have spoken to you, that My joy may remain in you, and that your joy may be full.*
>
> —John 15:11

Jesus finishes this teaching on prayer, and the fruit that comes forth from the indwelling Word allows you to ask whatever you desire, not just what you need. Needs and wants are two different things. A want is something you desire. Therefore, you can ask what you desire, and you will get it.

This verse says, "My joy will remain in you, and your joy will be full." As I understand it, the word *full* means to "be replenished, overflowing." There will never be a time when it goes below the rim. It will always be to the top and overflowing. The fulfillment of that kind of promise comes from a continual relationship with God. Therefore, you should always be in outflow. If you are not, it indicates that you're encountering weakness and you're humble and contrite, and the cycle starts again.

God comes to dwell with those who are humble and contrite, but the Word also says, "He will heal your broken heart." He will revive you and give you courage in your contriteness. This is the process of walking it out. Most people don't go past this step. They don't get to the counsel of God where they are shown, like the Laodiceans, that they are blind, naked, and poor. They don't even get to that place with the Lord. Once you receive this, you walk in humility in need of God to show you, help you, and heal you. He will show you His faithfulness.

He is the high and lofty One, but He also dwells with those who are humble and contrite in spirit. After this, you will experience healing. You will receive restoration, and from there, you will manifest the power and love of God so people can see the fruit. The fruit of the Spirit will be evident, and His joy will remain in you to the fullest.

PRAYER:

Father, in the name of Jesus, thank You for everything You have done. I thank You for all those reading this book. I pray that they would receive every impartation of the Spirit that You have for them, in the name of Jesus. Let the light of the gospel be evident right now, in the name of Jesus. Amen.

May you continue to live a full life in the counsel of God and discover all that He desires to reveal to you. May you live a life of obedience and righteousness unto the Lord, and may He grant favor to you for your surrendered heart to Him.

Take time with the Lord to pray and seek intimacy with Him. Invite His counsel to minister to you on the various points discussed in this book.

Appendix

God Counsels *as* You Lead

So Moses' father-in-law said to him, "The thing that you do is not good. Both you and these people who are with you will surely wear yourselves out. For this thing is too much for you; you are not able to perform it by yourself. Listen now to my voice; I will give you counsel, and God will be with you: Stand before God for the people, so that you may bring the difficulties to God. And you shall teach them the statutes and the laws, and show them the way in which they must walk and the work they must do.

—Exodus 18:17–20

MOSES was known for his deep connection with God. He encountered many spiritual manifestations in his time of counsel with Him. One of these occurred when Moses was counseling people in the desert, almost five million people. You can imagine what it is like dealing with a small group of people and all that occurs in their everyday lives. Think about how you would handle the disputes of nearly five million people.

So Moses's father-in-law came to him and said, "This is not good. It's going to wear you out." His father-in-law had to counsel him on how to deal with his current situation of judging between the people. He then instructed Moses to present his difficulties to God so that he would know what to do and teach them the laws and statutes.

Moses's father-in-law directed him to select God-fearing men of truth to be rulers and judges over the people. This was so they could bear the burdens, allowing Moses to focus on the larger issues and also free him up to be in counsel with God and lead effectively.

As a leader, when you have the counsel of God with wisdom and impartation, you need more support to oversee many people. The key is to stay in communion with God and hear His voice so He can help and guide you so that you can be a great leader. However, to manage and do a great job with a larger group of people, you must impart the same spirit and knowledge that you carry to others. Moses would have become ineffective if he hadn't raised other men to lead under him.

The solution came through Moses's father-in-law so that the people who oversaw the ministry then had that intimacy of counsel. Moses chose trusted people, able men who feared God. Some of these men were over groups of ten, and others were over groups of hundreds and thousands. They answered to Moses, but they answered to each other in that chain of command.

For example, what happened to me was similar; I was plucked out, taken to Heaven, shown heavenly realities, and then sent back. My job is not to talk about my experience and only teach; it is to impart it to others so they can also carry it. If you can hand off your teaching in this way, your outreach and influence will be much more effective. The goal is to find people you can trust, people who are able and who fear God, love truth, and hate covetousness. It was not easy when people did not encounter God as Moses did. It was God's will that they experienced what Moses was encountering, but they were rebellious. All of this had to happen because it became God's will.

The men Moses chose judged the people, so Moses didn't have to manage all the cases and disputes. This approach allowed for better conflict management by putting people in a position to handle it. Warrior Notes has implemented this biblical approach.

Today, we are utilizing my experience of being caught up, then implementing and teaching it, writing books, and teaching classes through Warrior Notes School of Ministry. Eventually, our students can teach people how to operate in these same truths and disciple people. They will be over the tens, fifties, hundreds, and thousands. In other words, you speak the truth in love and allow people to become more Christlike. You continue to help and manage your area under your realm of influence. This is God's plan. Then, the burden is taken off me to do this with the hundreds of thousands of people we're influencing. It is easier when you have other people to help carry the load.

The plan is to make disciples after you are caught up in the counsel of God. We see how Paul made disciples. People were under Paul, then they became pastors and part of the church. The church grew from there. That is how it will be here at Warrior Notes.

AN OBEDIENT AND HOLY NATION

> *For they had departed from Rephidim, had come to the Wilderness of Sinai, and camped in the wilderness. So Israel camped there before the mountain. And Moses went up to God, and the Lord called to him from the mountain, saying, "Thus you shall say to the house of Jacob, and tell the children of Israel: 'You have seen what I did to the Egyptians, and how I bore you on eagles' wings and brought you to Myself. Now therefore, if you will indeed obey My voice and keep My*

covenant, then you shall be a special treasure to Me above all people; for all the earth is Mine.'"

—Exodus 19:2–5

Jesus echoed this same language in John 14:15 when He said, "If you love Me, keep My commandments." You show Jesus that you love Him by obeying Him. When you do, you will be a special treasure above all.

'And you shall be to Me a kingdom of priests and a holy nation.' These are the words which you shall speak to the children of Israel."

—Exodus 19:6

In this passage, God is talking about Israel as a kingdom of priests. They are all priests and a holy nation, a set apart people. Moses received this counsel and then imparted it to the people. It is incredible how good the people had it with God. They encountered the supernatural every day. Daily, millions of people received manna from Heaven and water from the rock. Yet their hearts were hardened, and they did not act as they were supposed to toward God. We do not realize how good the children of Israel had it, but so do we. We have it even better, and we do not discern it.

Since I encountered the other side and was sent back, I see these matters as black and white. It is apparent to me, but it is not easy to teach this to others. That is how it was with Moses. However, it was his job to deliver the message in Exodus 19 where God said, "You tell the people that if they will hear my voice and obey it, that I will make them my special treasure and that I will promote them above all the people on the earth."

The people of Israel were supposed to be priests and a holy nation. In the new covenant, the Most High God has promoted us to be priests and kings. When this is not preached, we all suffer. We all need to hear what Moses heard and implement it in our lives as the people in his day should have. We saw what happened to them.

The book of Hebrews describes the people who fell in the desert because of their disobedience and hardened hearts due to unbelief (Hebrews 3:12–19). They didn't enter the promised land because the promises were conditional. So they didn't become God's treasure nor did they become the priests in the holy nation that God said they were.

We hear the Word of God, respond to it, implement it, and encounter it by faith. This is all done by the counsel transferred from God to Moses, then from Moses to the elders, and from the elders to the people. This has been the setup from the beginning.

Salvation Prayer

Lord God,

I confess that I am a sinner.

I confess that I need Your Son, Jesus.

Please forgive me in His Name.

Lord Jesus, I believe You died for me and that You

are alive and listening to me now.

I now turn from my sins and

welcome You into my heart.

Come and take control of my life.

Make me the kind of person You want me to be.

Now, fill me with Your Holy Spirit,

who will show me how to live for You.

I acknowledge You before men as

my Savior and my Lord.

In Jesus's name. Amen.

If you prayed this prayer,
please get in touch with us at

info@kevinzadai.com
for more information and material.

We welcome you to join our network at
warriornotes.tv for access to
exclusive programming.

To enroll in our ministry school, go to:
www.warriornotesschool.com

Visit **www.kevinzadai.com** for
additional ministry materials.

About Dr. Kevin Zadai

KEVIN Zadai, PhD, was called to the ministry at the age of ten. He attended Central Bible College in Springfield, Missouri, where he received a Bachelor of Arts in theology. Later, he received training in missions at Rhema Bible College, a ThD from Primus University, and a PhD from Life Christian University. Dr. Kevin L. Zadai is dedicated to training Christians to live and operate in two realms simultaneously—the supernatural and the natural.

At age thirty-one, Kevin met Jesus in Heaven, got a second chance at life, and received a revelation that he could not fail because it is all rigged in our favor! Kevin holds a commercial pilot license and is retired from Southwest Airlines after twenty-nine years as a flight attendant. He is the founder and president of Warrior Notes School of Ministry. He and his lovely wife, Kathi, reside in New Orleans, Louisiana.

Warrior Tunes

Access Kevin Zadai's complete audio library anytime, anywhere with Warrior Tunes. Stream directly on your phone or computer.

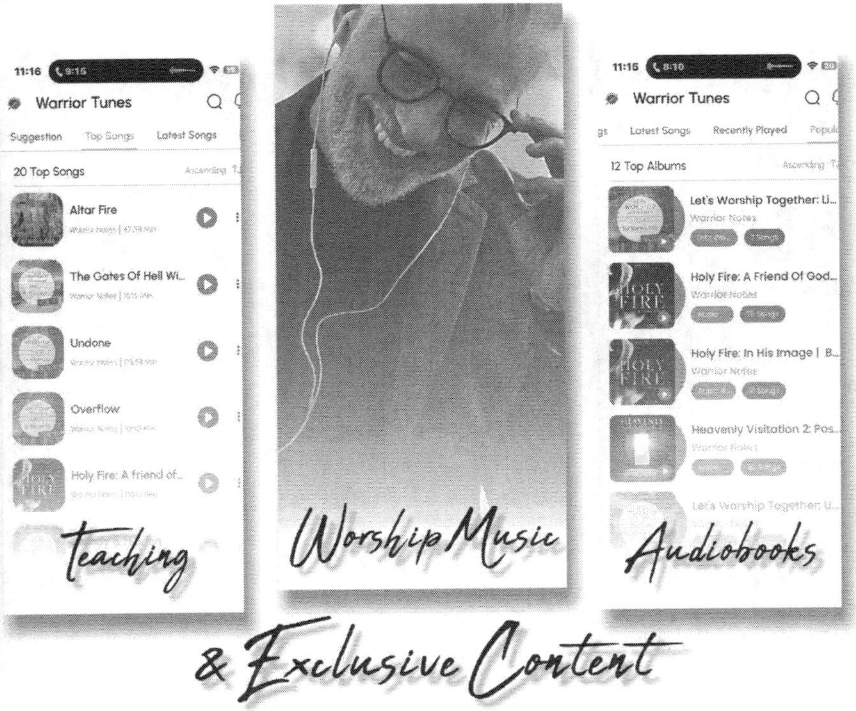

Scan the QR for more information about Warrior Tunes, or visit:
warriortunes.com

Warrior Fellowships

Join a local Warrior Fellowship—where powerful teaching meets local community impact through…

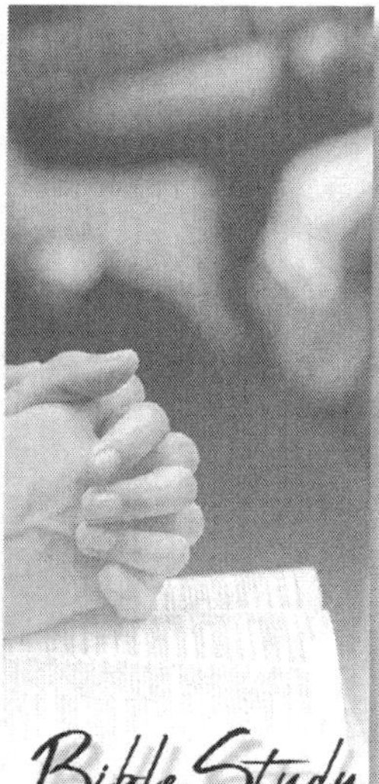

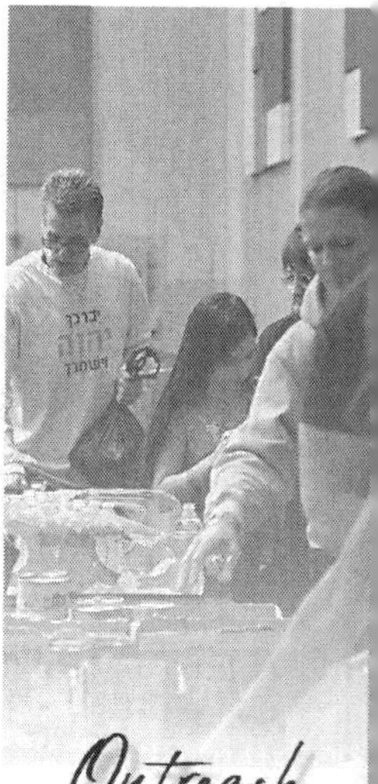

Scan the QR for more information about a Warrior Fellowship near you, or visit:
warriorchurches.netviewshop.com/contact

Warrior Notes Regional Events

Experience transformative teaching, outreach, and mentoring at one of our upcoming **Spirit Schools.** You will deepen your spiritual journey through intensive biblical instruction, hands-on ministry training, and connection with like-minded believers.

Visit **kevinzadai.com/events/**
to see where WN will be next.